Board Silly
on the Coast

Surf Cartoons and Journal

CF Greenstein

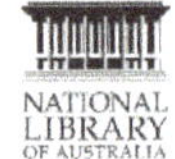

A catalogue record for this book is available from the National Library of Australia

ISBN-13: 978-1-923174-69-6

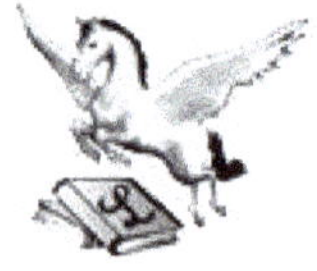

Linellen Press
265 Boomerang Road
Oldbury, Western Australia
helen.linpress@gmail.com

Dedication

For my surf buddies, especially the Spring Chickens crew, whose antics in and out of the surf formed a rich source of material. Their endless good humour prompted me to make cartoons of our experiences and motivated me to share the humour.

For my swim buddies and other friends, whose encouragement and support were so helpful in navigating the project.

Finally, for all the other aquatic creatures who enjoy a laugh and a wave. You know who you are!

Contents

How to Use This Journal

There are many ways to keep a journal. As the cartoons in this book have a surf theme, one might use it as a surf journal to note great surf locations, a particular set of conditions at a favourite break, achievements, goals, or reflections on how one surfed on a given day.

Ideal Surf Conditions

Wave height and direction _2-3 feet, right hand_
Swell height and direction _5 feet E_
Wind speed and direction _3 kph, SW_
Tide _mid-tide dropping_
Other _when Venus aligns with Mars!_

Alternatively, one might use the book as a general journal or appointment notebook.

A journal is what you make it.

I have included a few ideas in the next two pages for those who might want a prompt. I have left the rest of the pages blank to document, sketch or reflect as one sees fit. There is a blank page for at least every week of the year.

| DATE |
| TIME |
| LOCATION |

SURF CONDITIONS
Wave Height and Direction
Swell Height and Direction
Wind Speed and Direction
Wave Period
Tide Height and Stage
Wave Energy
Consistency
Water Temperature

ENVIRONMENT
Local Vibe
Crowd Factor
Access to beach and parking
Hazards
Water Quality
Rubbish
Bottom

SURF LOG
Duration of Surf Session
Number of Waves
Longest Ride
Moves Worked On

LOCAL KNOWLEDGE
Ideal tides
Sandbanks
Rips
Seasonal Factors

EQUIPMENT
Surfboard Size and Type
Fin Type and set up
Clothing

REFLECTIONS
Things that went well
Things that did not go well
Things to work on
Mood Check

Sketch of Local Break

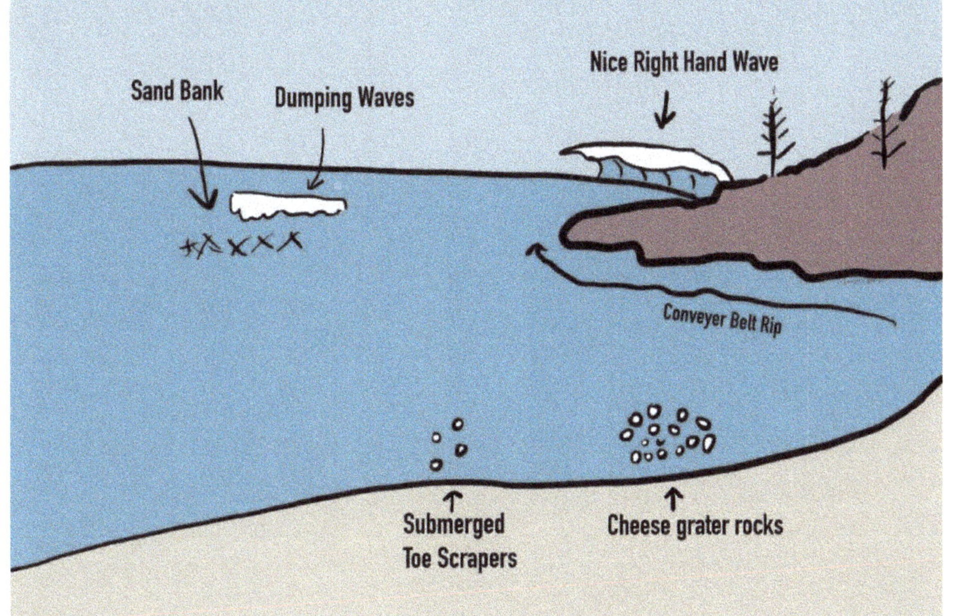

A Guide to Local Surf Waves

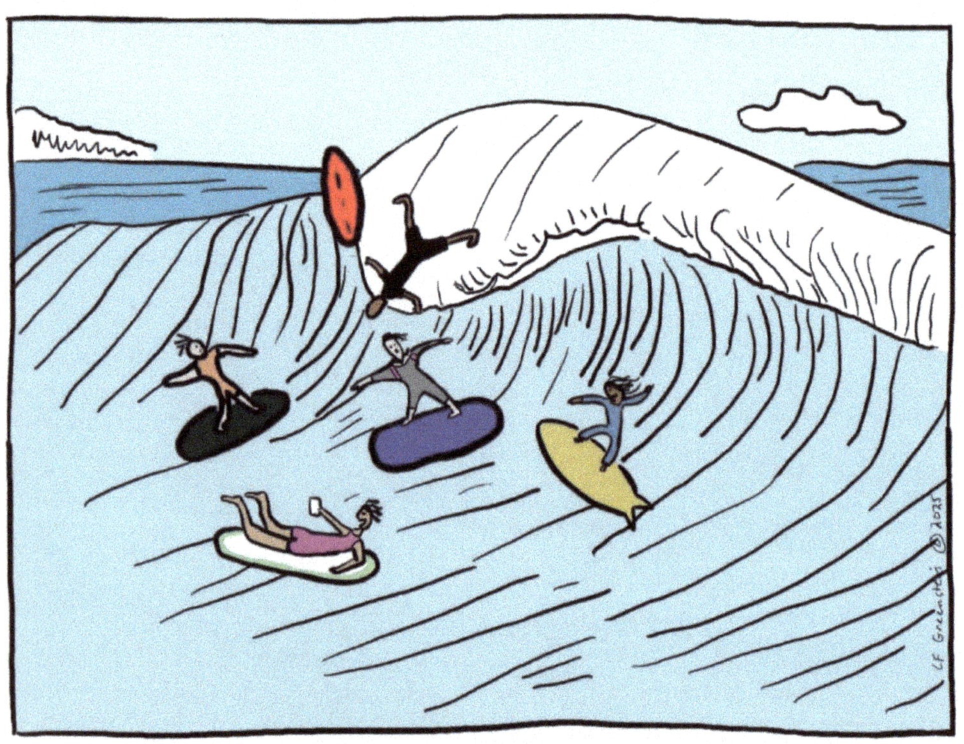

The Rush Hour Wave

The wave seen prior to school or work and on weekends notable for the number of surfers riding, paddling around and floating on it.

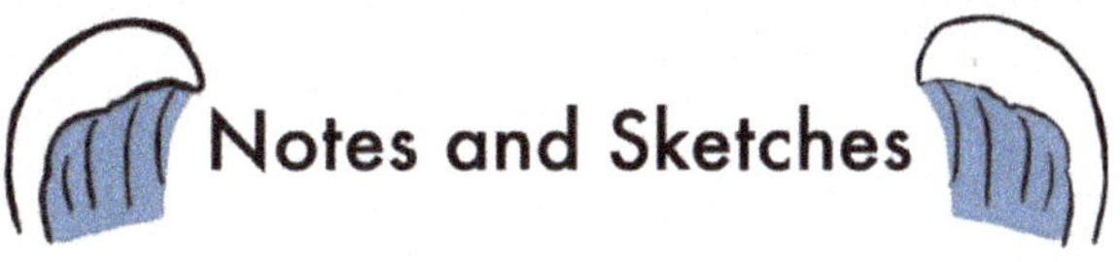

Notes and Sketches

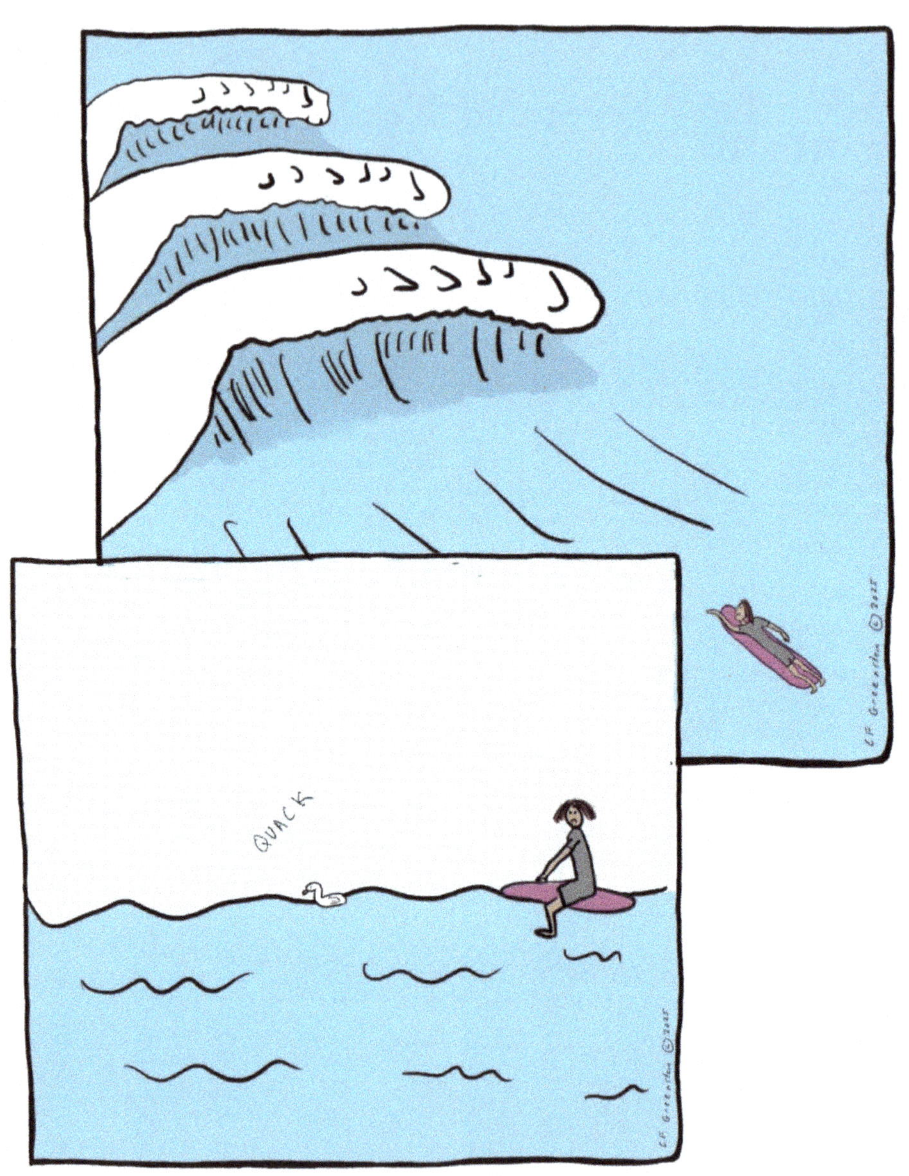

The Mirage Wave
The imaginary wave one sees in the distance
and paddles to only to find it doesn't exist.

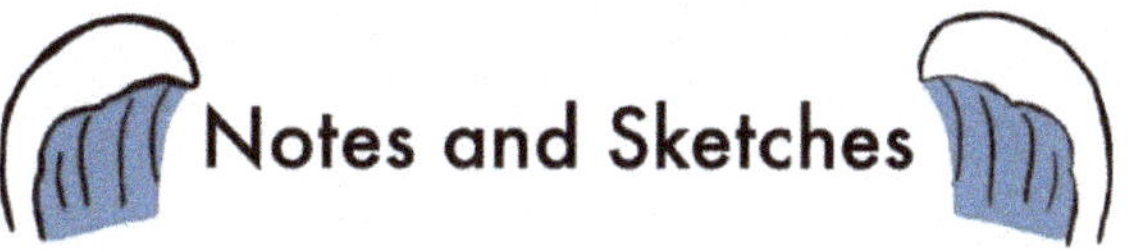

Notes and Sketches

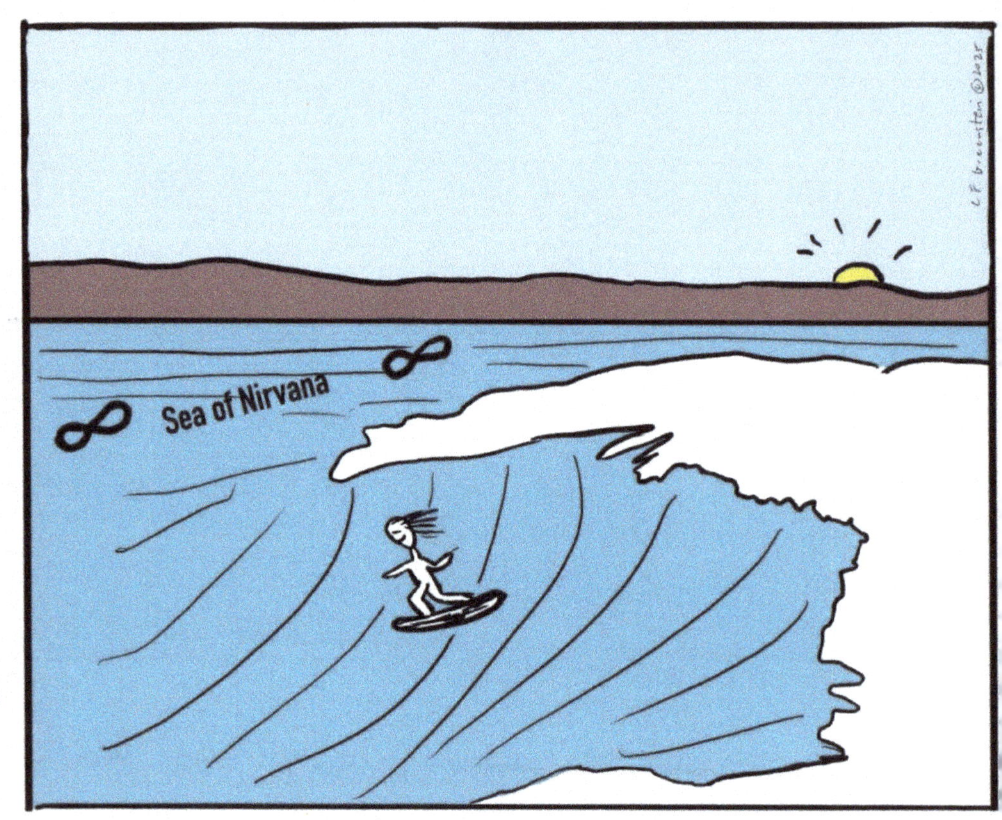

The Lover Wave

The wave that is soft, strong and supportive offering
excitement with little drama.

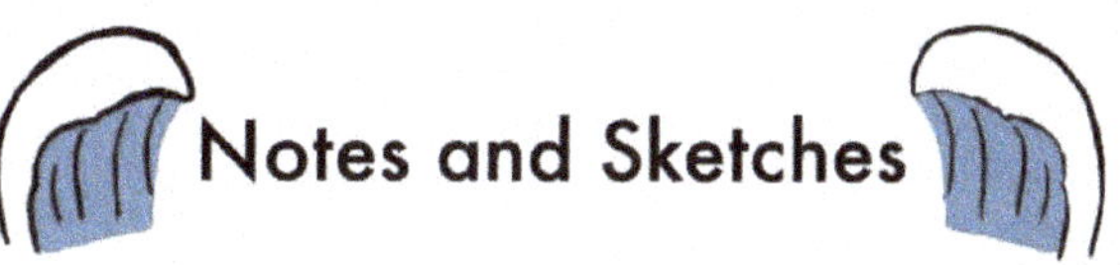

Notes and Sketches

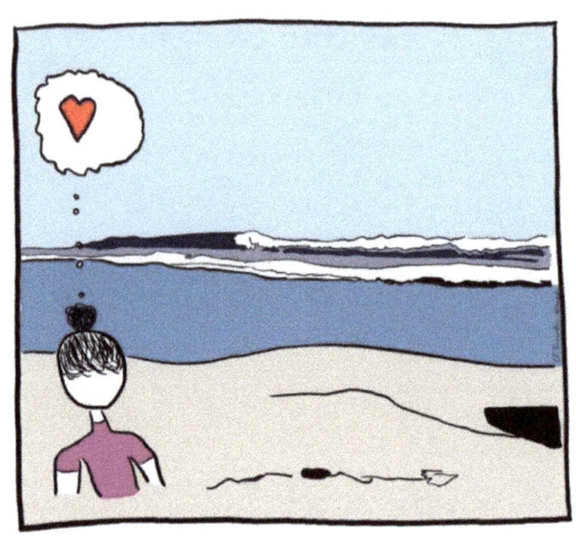

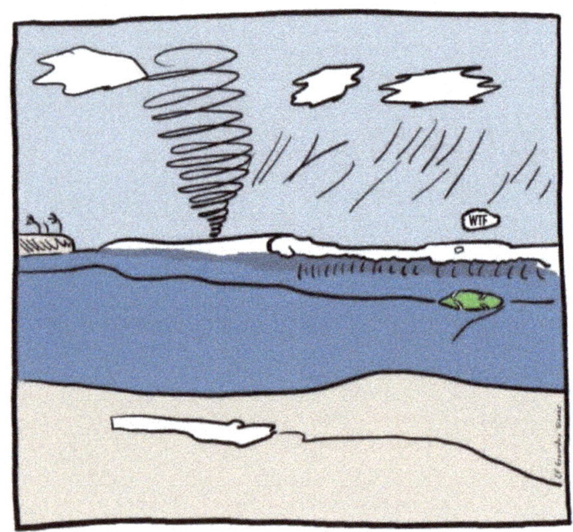

The Ex-Lover Wave

The perfect wave that beckons from the shore...
but feels like a category 5 cyclone when you paddle out.

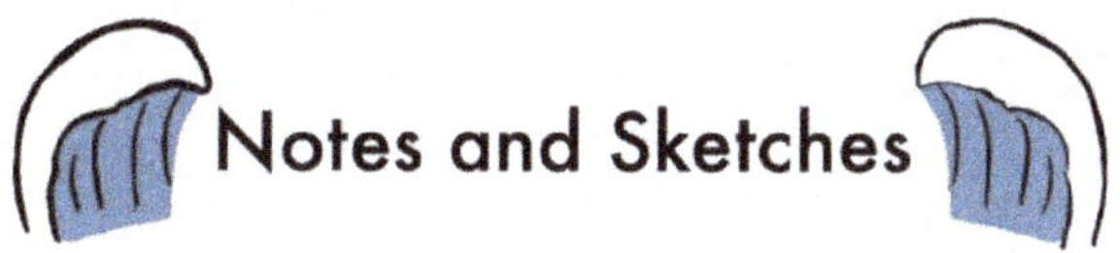

Notes and Sketches

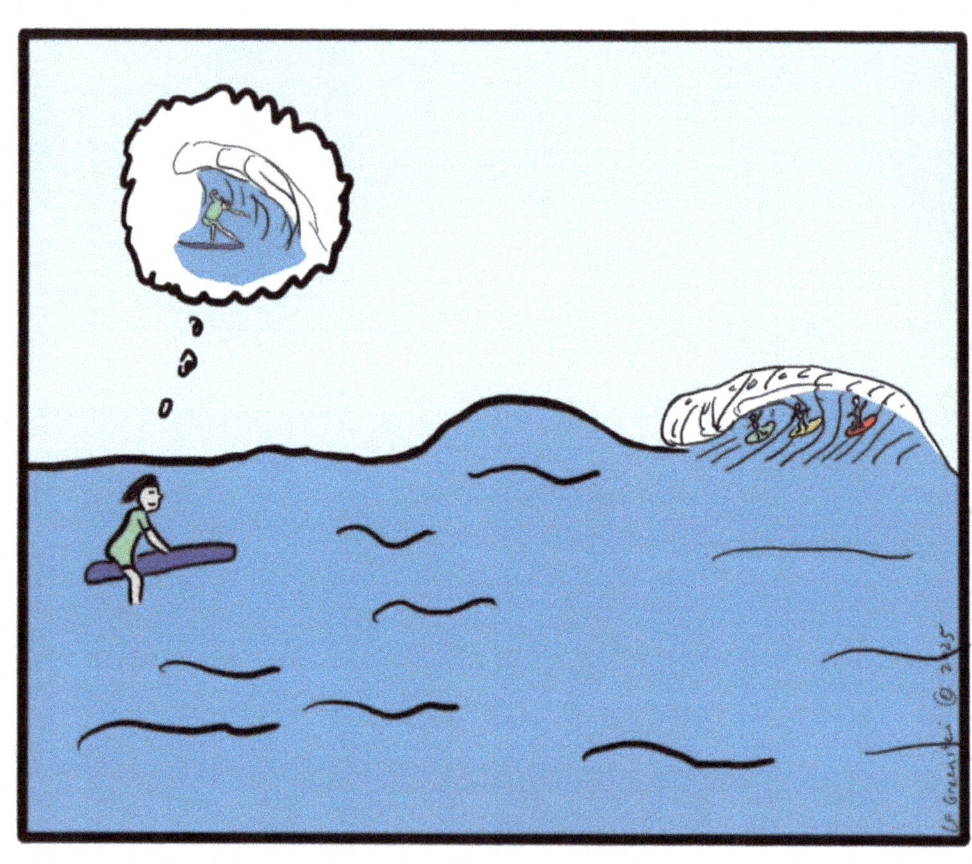

The Gone Fishing Wave

The wave you observe as you sit for hours far from the surf zone. Too far away to catch anything, you dream of "the one that got away".

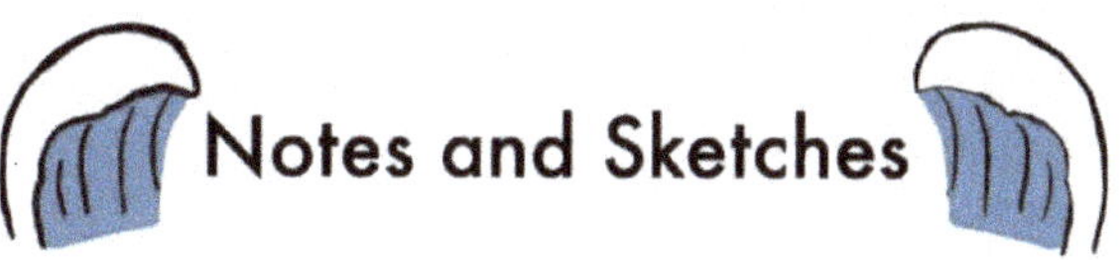

Notes and Sketches

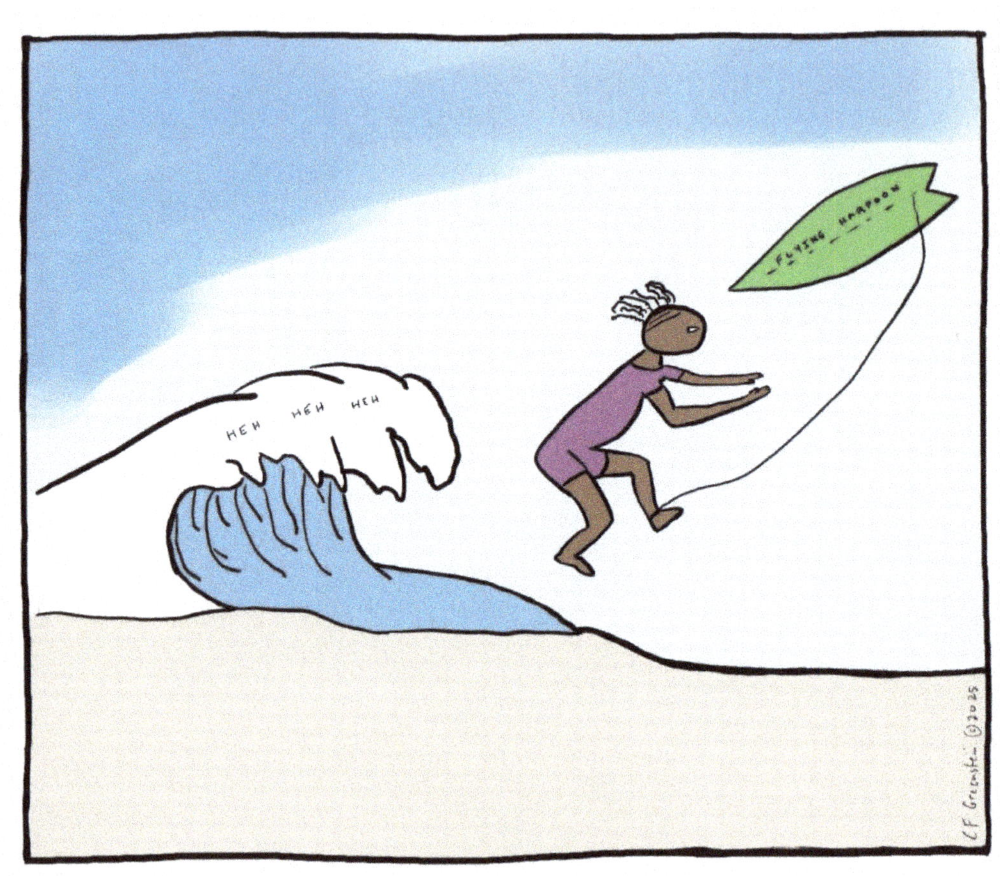

The Rogue Wave

**The wave that smacks you on the butt and
knocks you over as you exit the surf.**

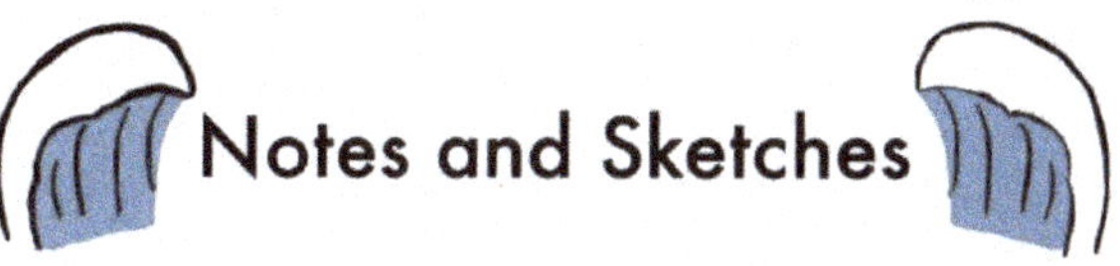

Notes and Sketches

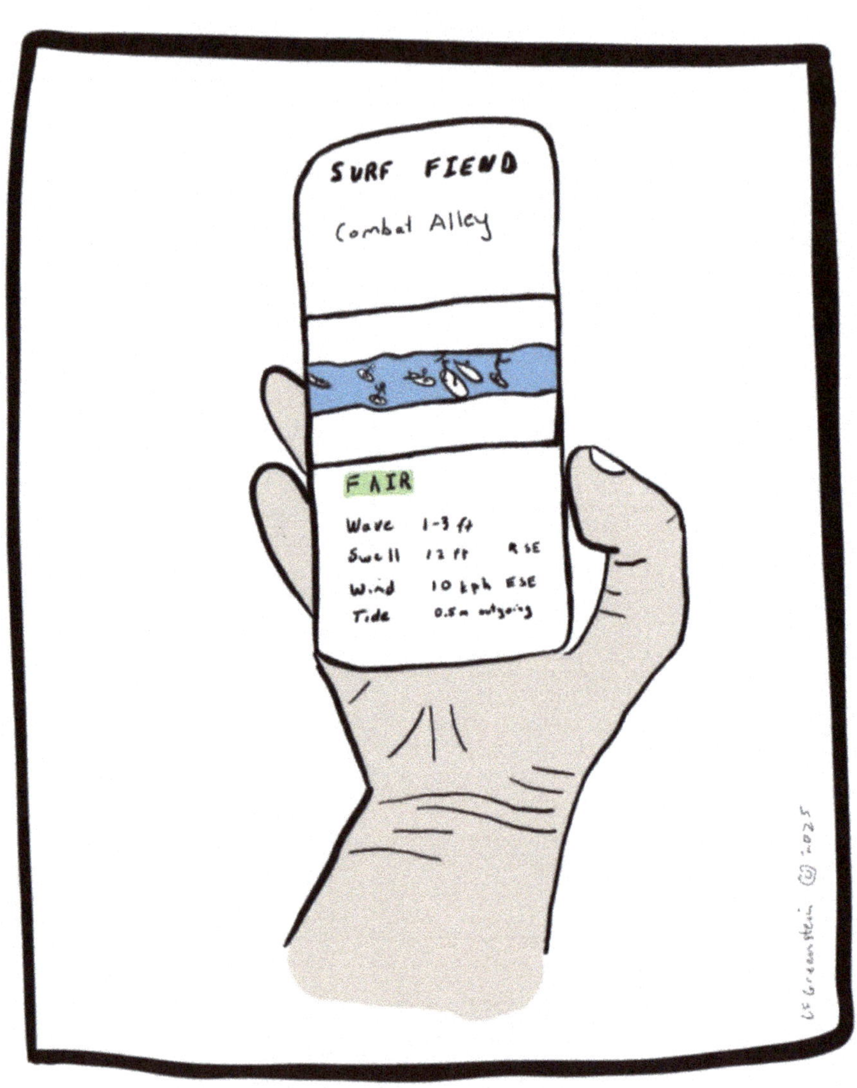

The Virtual Wave

The wave you view on your smartphone surf app when at
work or doing some chore.

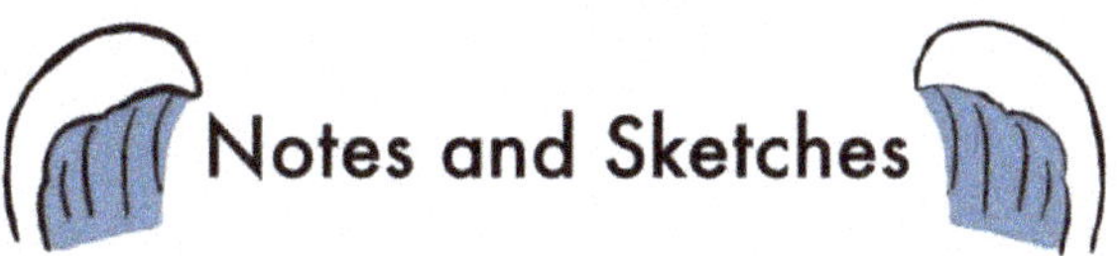

Notes and Sketches

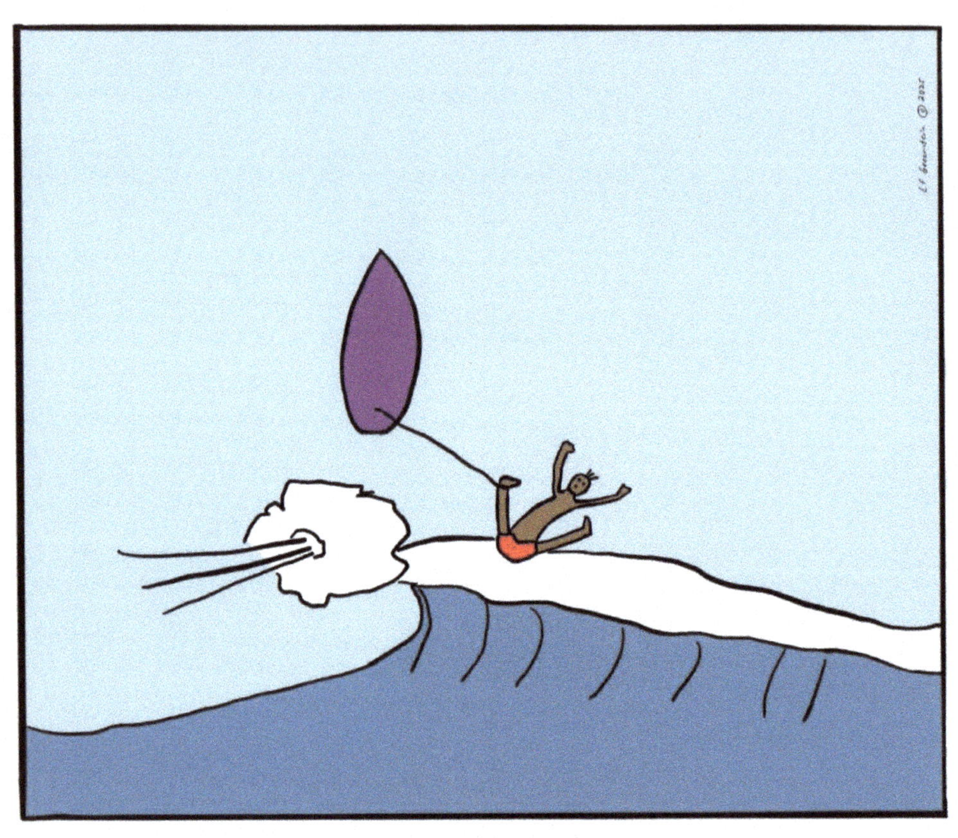

The Airbag Wave

The wave you catch when a strong offshore
wind arises and knocks you backwards.

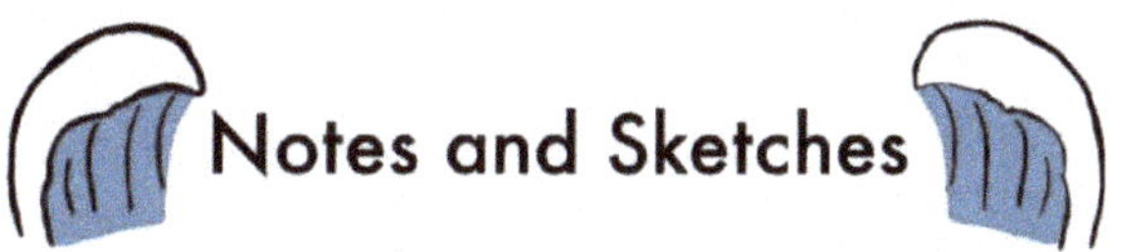

Notes and Sketches

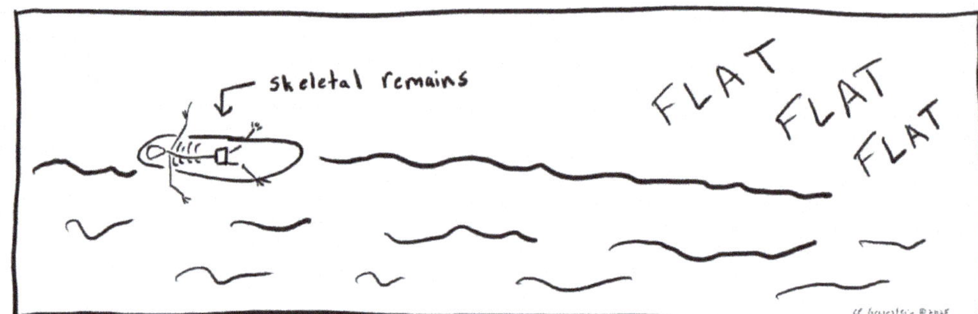

The Last Wave

The wave you look for to take you back to shore at the end of the session.

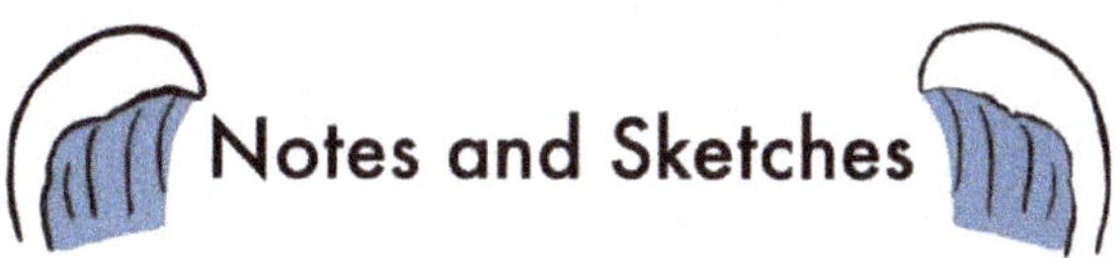

Notes and Sketches

WHEN GOOD SURF INSTRUCTORS GO BAD

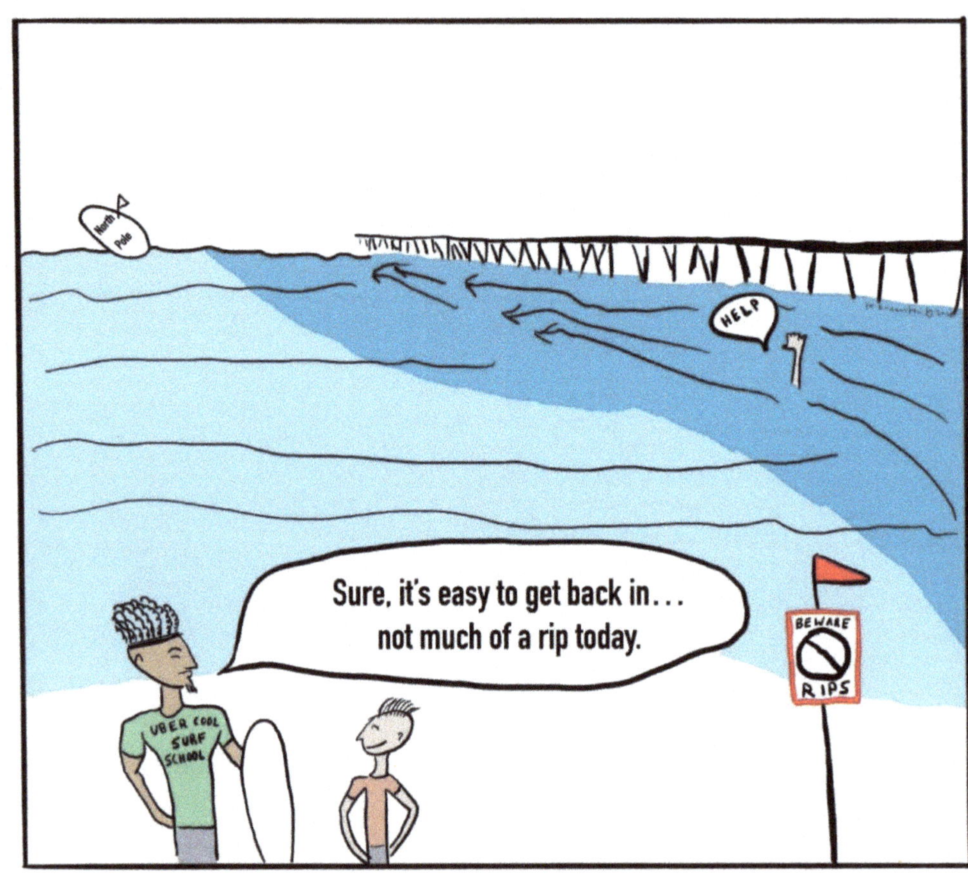

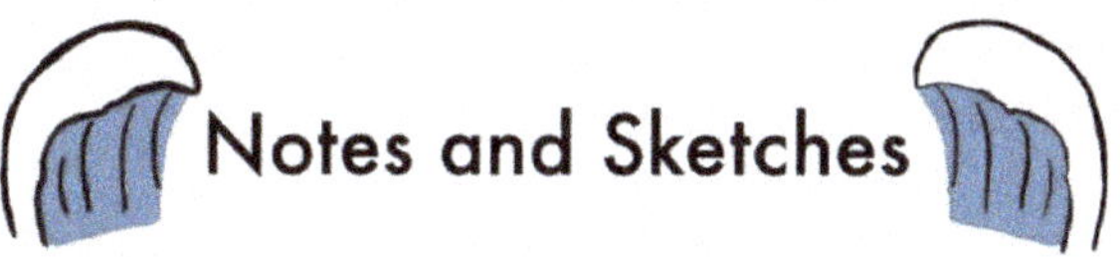

Notes and Sketches

WHEN GOOD SURF INSTRUCTORS GO BAD

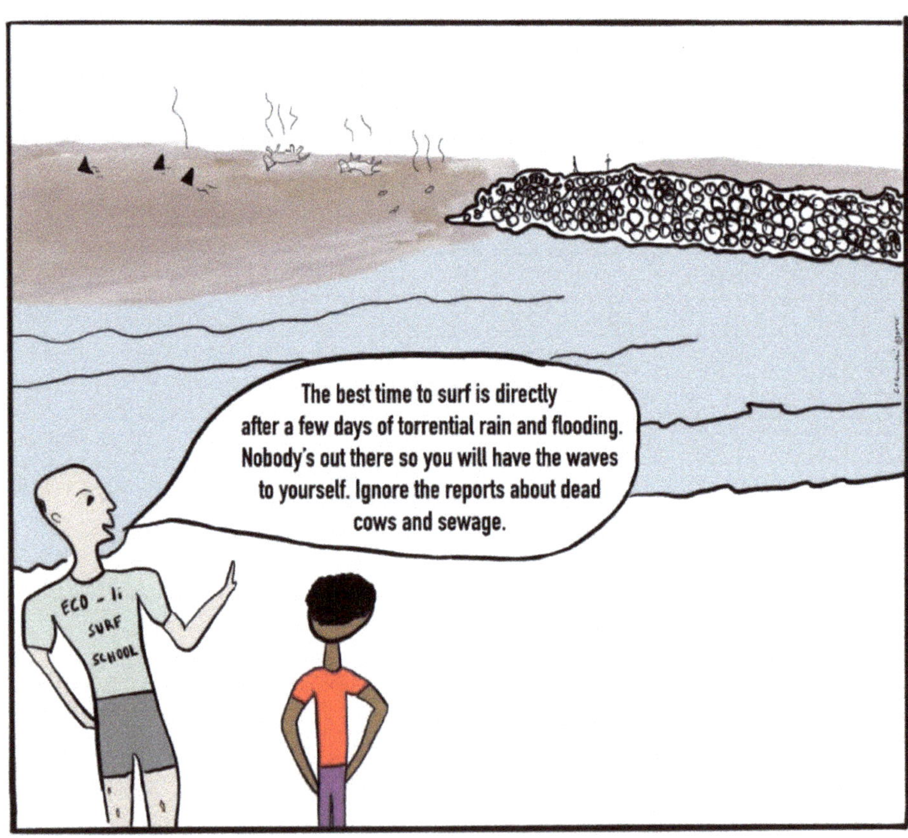

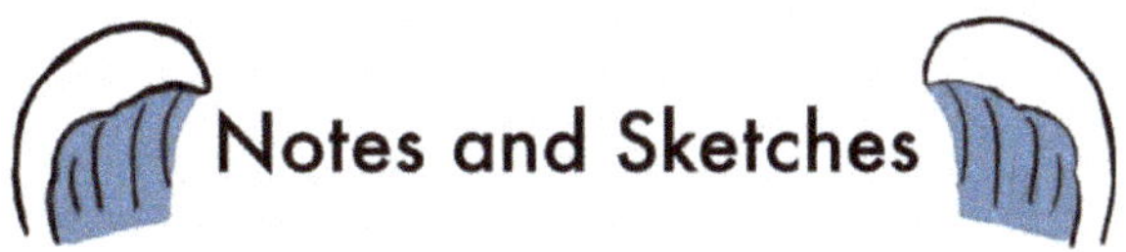
Notes and Sketches

WHEN GOOD SURF INSTRUCTORS GO BAD

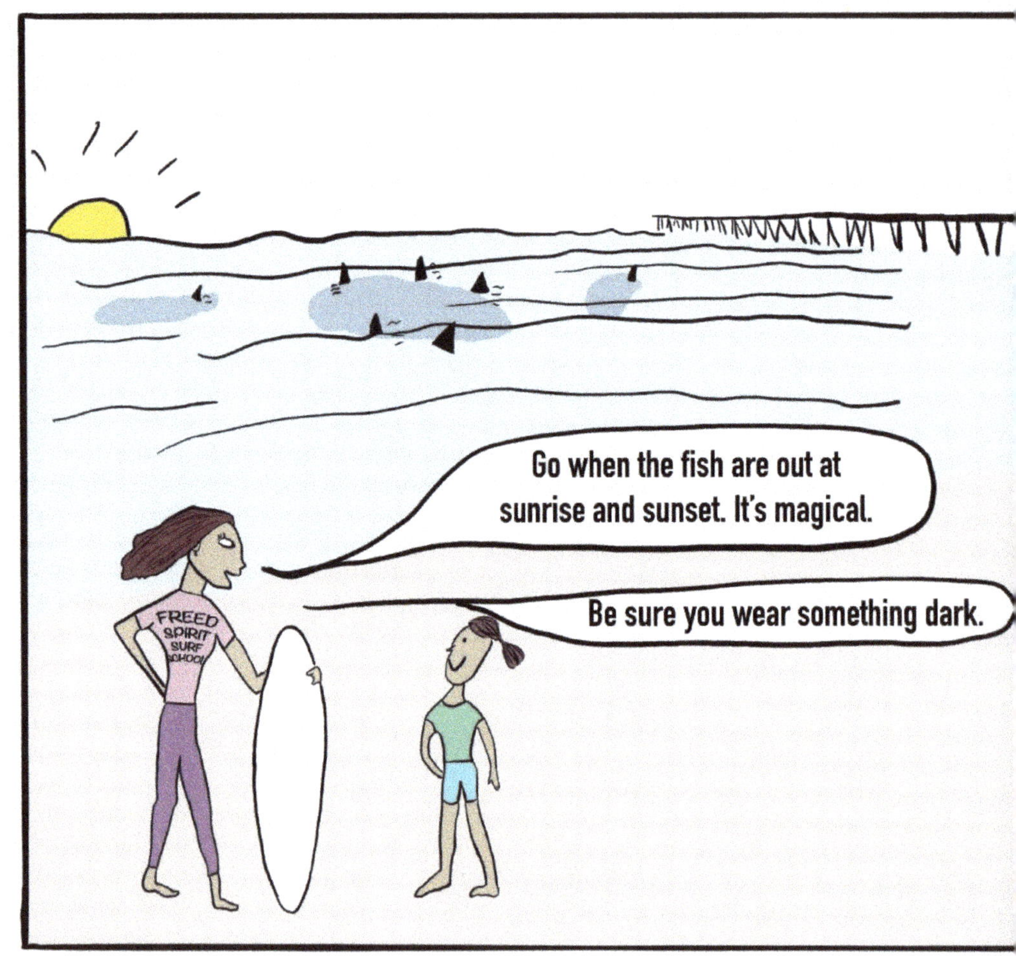

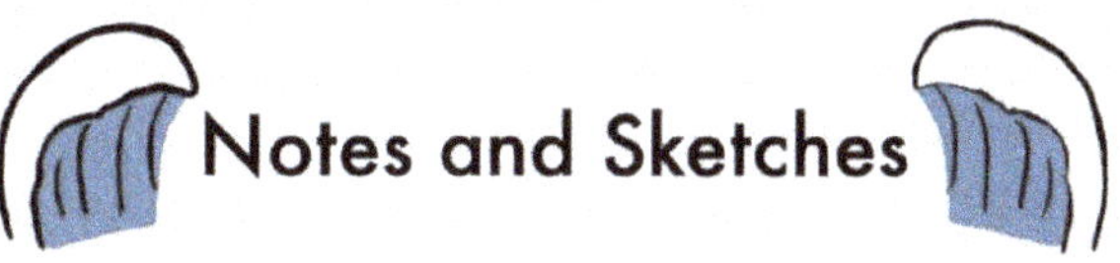

Notes and Sketches

WHEN GOOD SURF INSTRUCTORS GO BAD

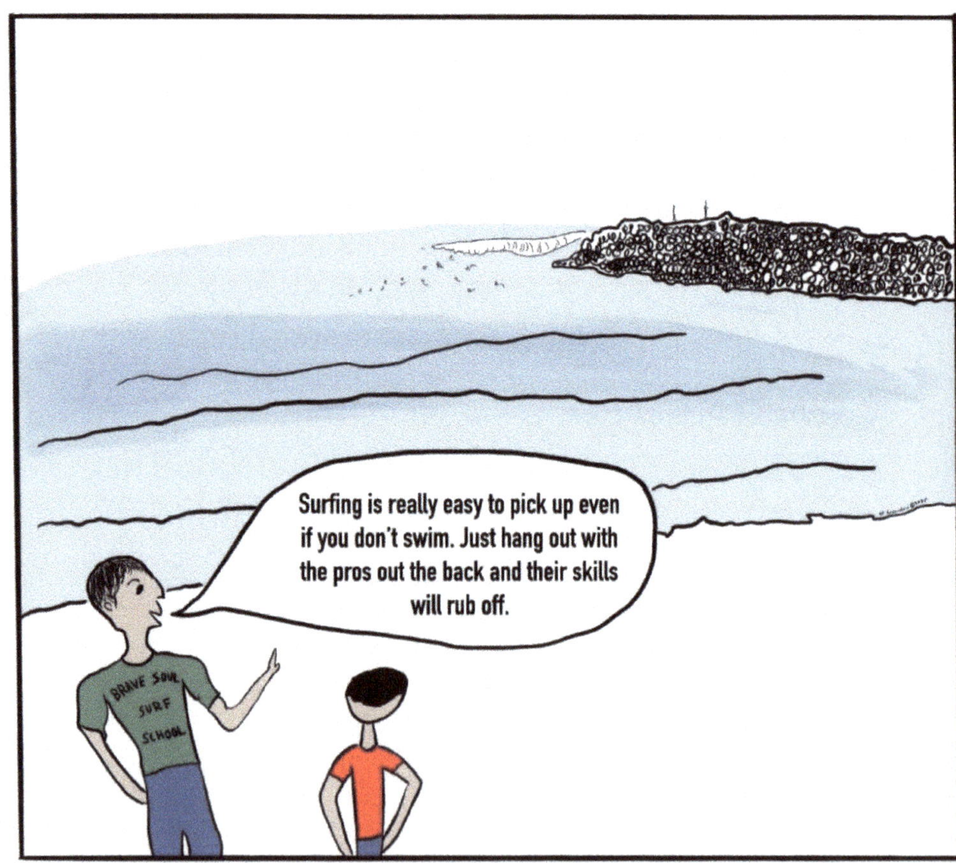

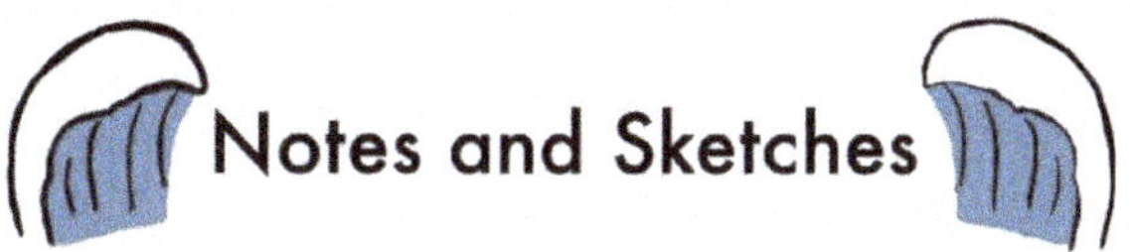

Notes and Sketches

Purchasing Mistakes Surfers Hate to Admit to...

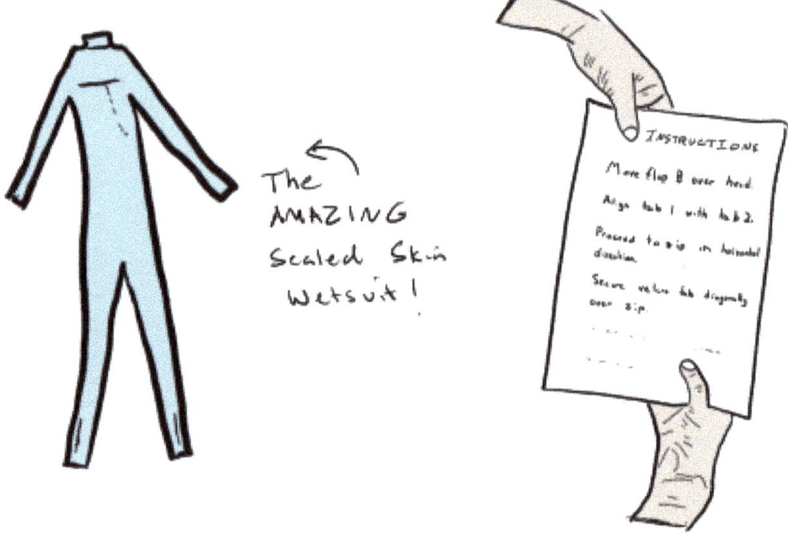

...buying a complicated wetsuit that is so snug it requires lubricant and a degree in engineering to put on.

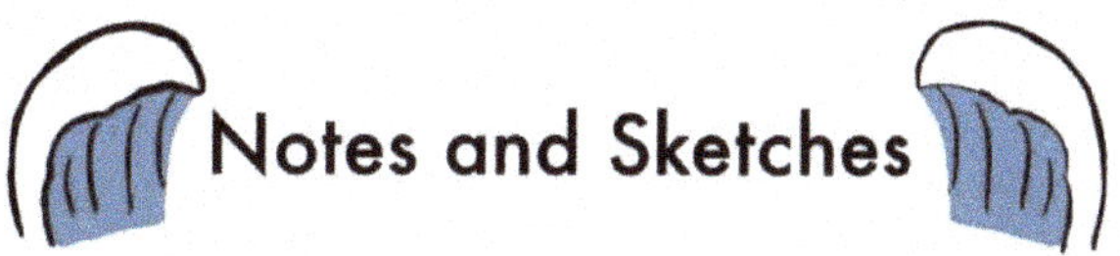

Notes and Sketches

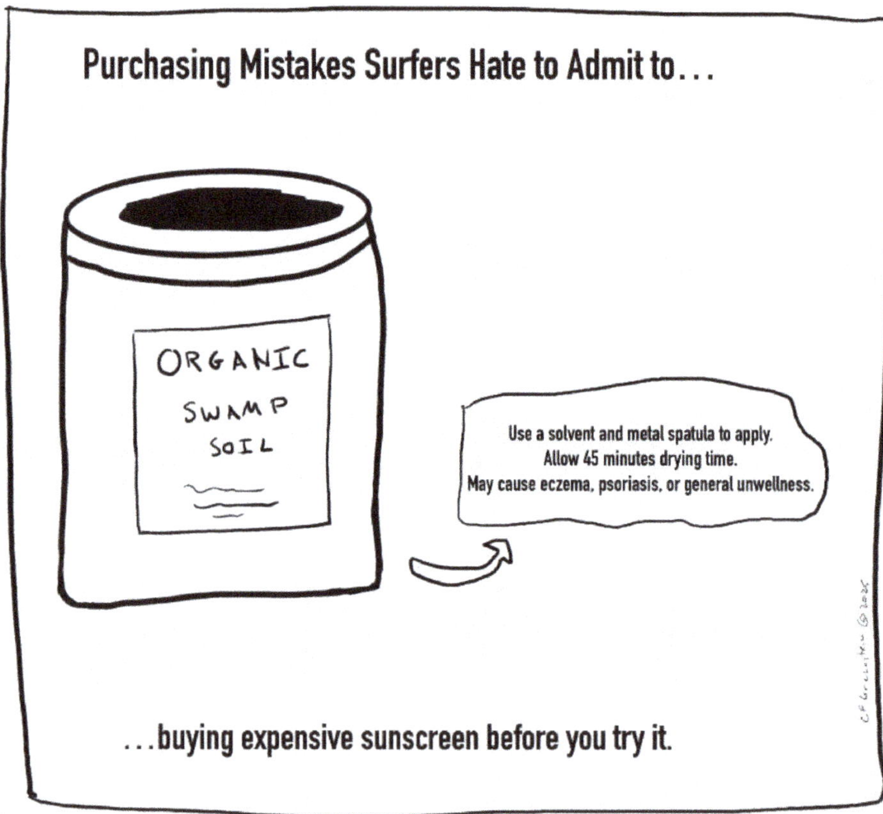

Purchasing Mistakes Surfers Hate to Admit to...
ORGANIC SWAMP SOIL
Use a solvent and metal spatula to apply.
Allow 45 minutes drying time.
May cause eczema, psoriasis, or general unwellness.
...buying expensive sunscreen before you try it.

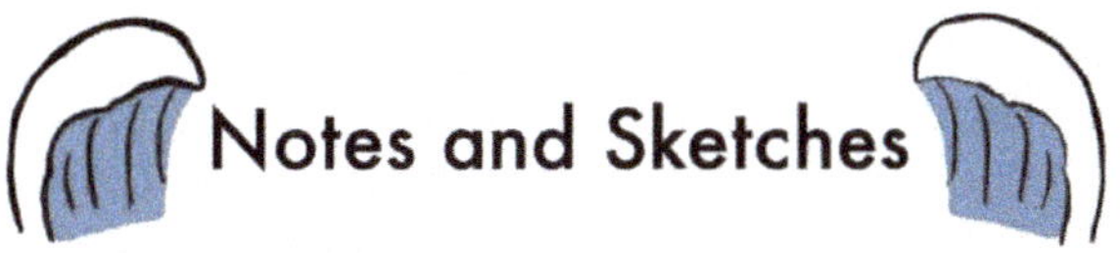
Notes and Sketches

Purchasing Mistakes Surfers Hate to Admit to...

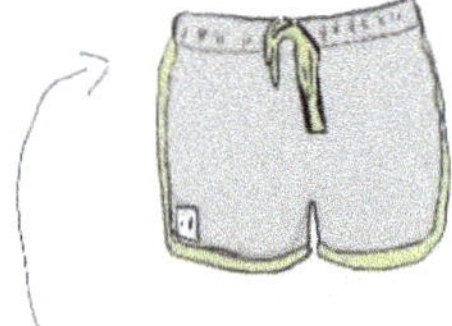

Ornamental tie sewed to front

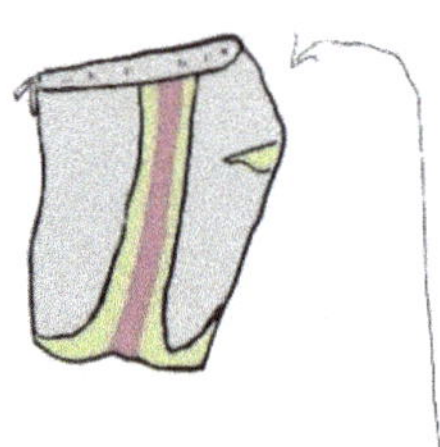

Elastic that goes slack at the hint of a wave.

...buying women's boardshorts that slip to your knees
when you wipe out.

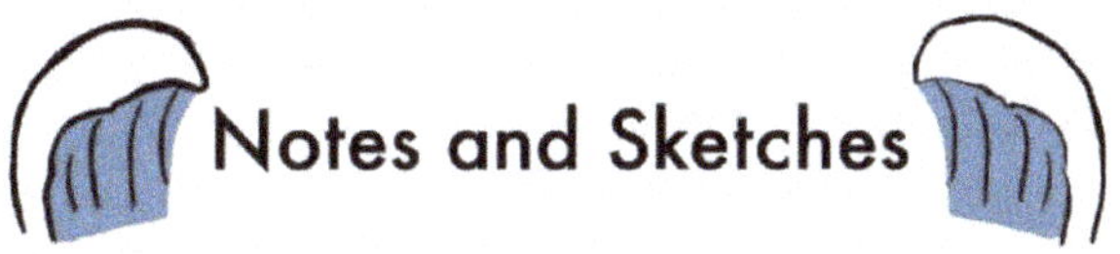

Notes and Sketches

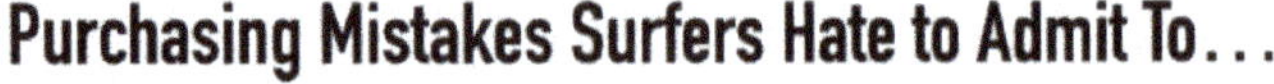

Purchasing Mistakes Surfers Hate to Admit To...

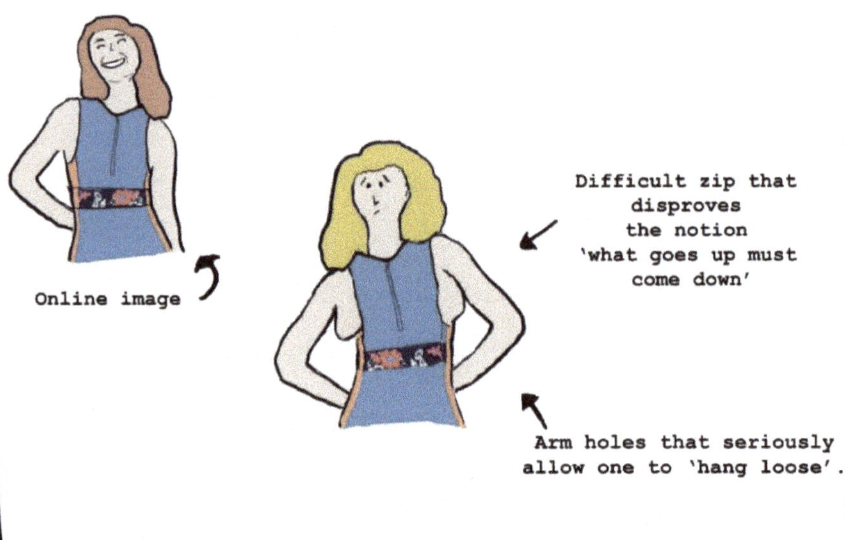

...buying surf wear online without trying it on first.

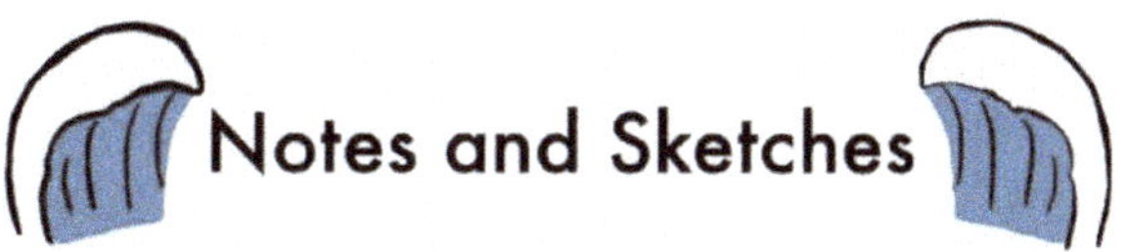
Notes and Sketches

Purchasing Mistakes Surfers Hate to Admit To...

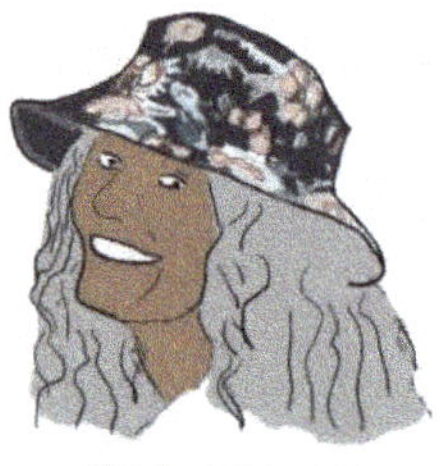

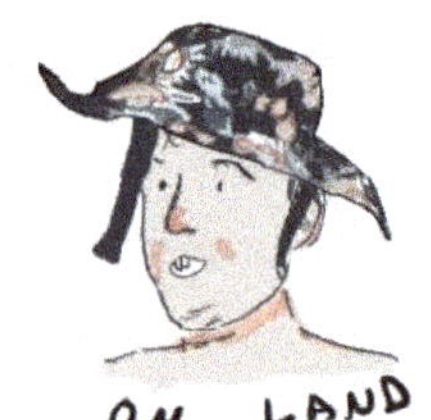

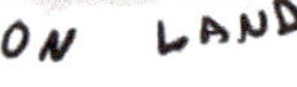

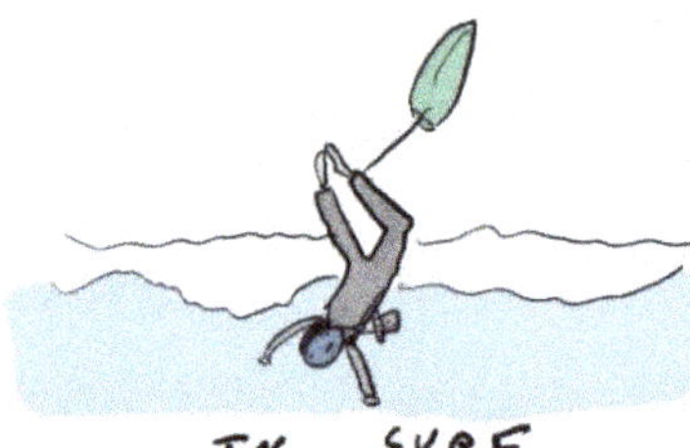

...buying that cute hat you saw online that makes you look like a drowned rat and strangles you in the surf.

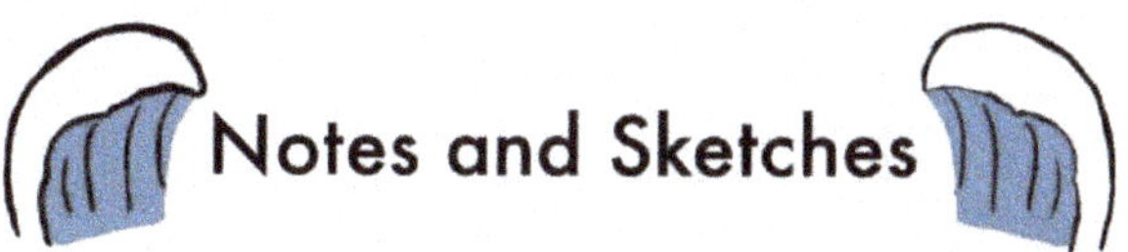

Notes and Sketches

How Not to Win Surfer Friends and Influence People

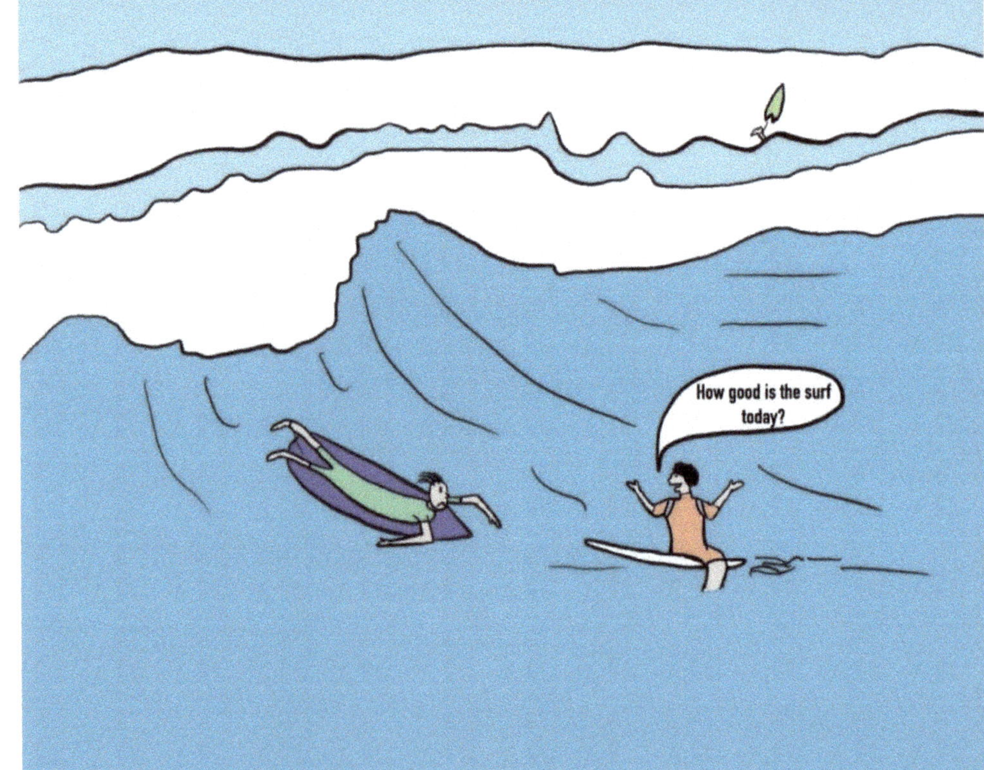

Paddle close to a surfer and start a conversation as a set of waves arrives.

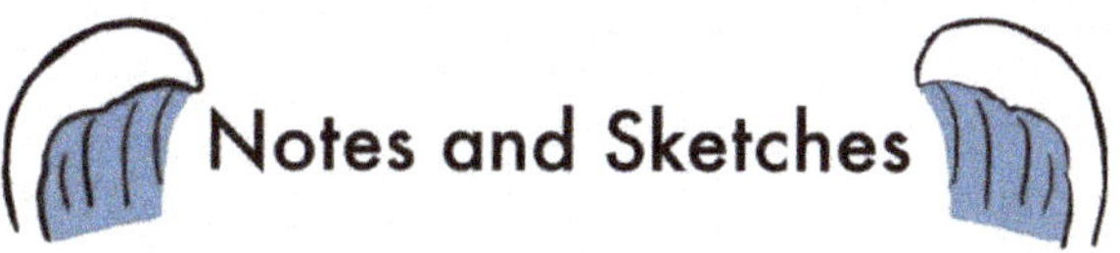

Notes and Sketches

How Not to Win Surfer Friends and Influence People

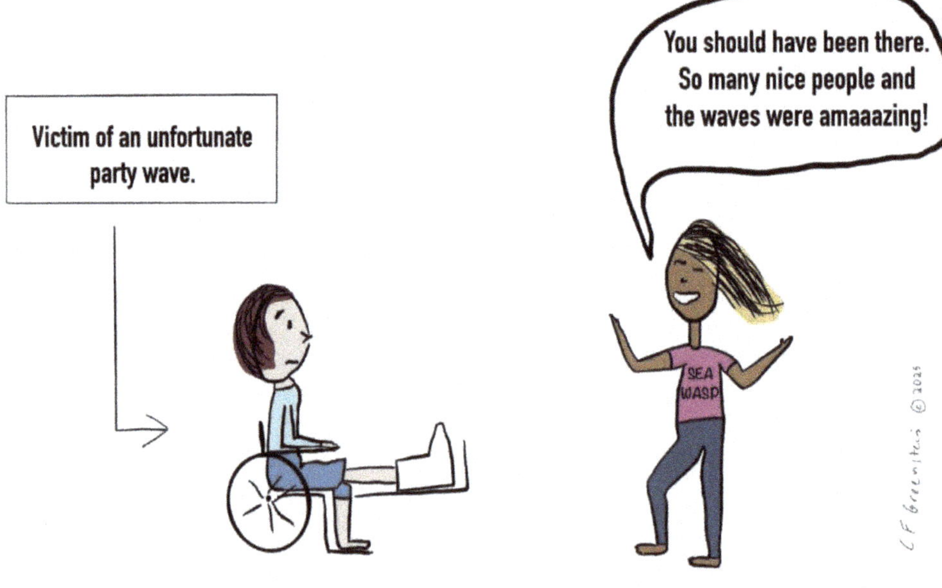

Overshare your joy with an incapacitated surfer.

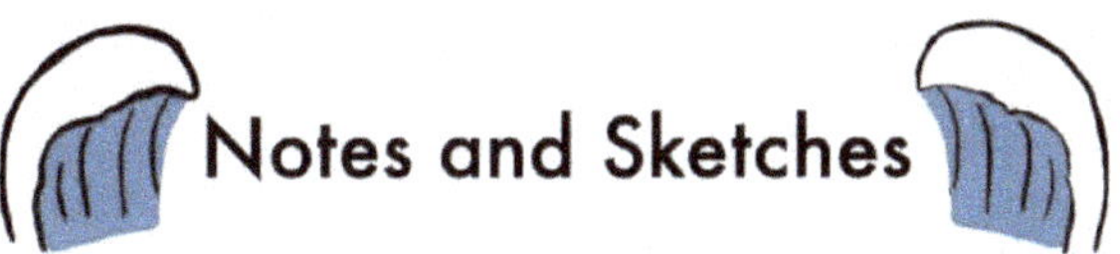
Notes and Sketches

How Not to Win Surfer Friends and Influence People

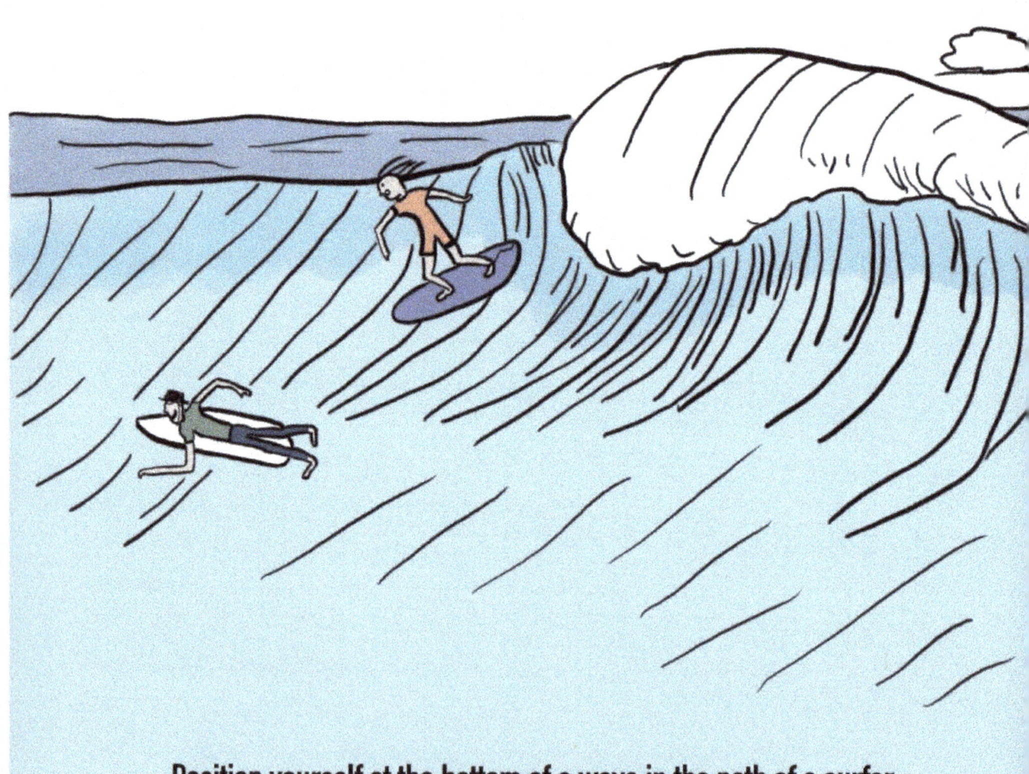

Position yourself at the bottom of a wave in the path of a surfer just in case she 'decides' not to take it.

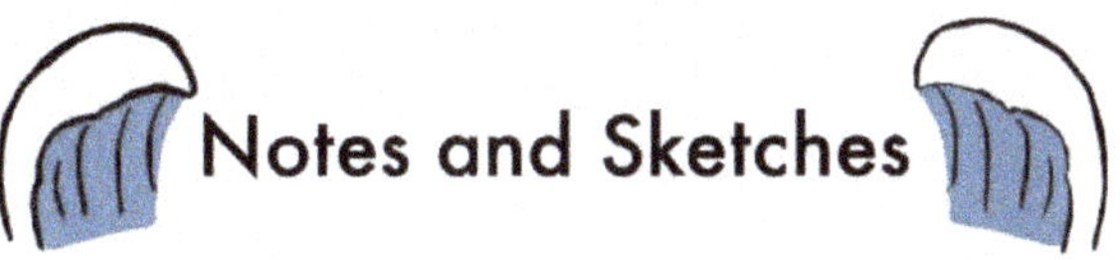

Notes and Sketches

How Not to Win Surfer Friends and Influence People

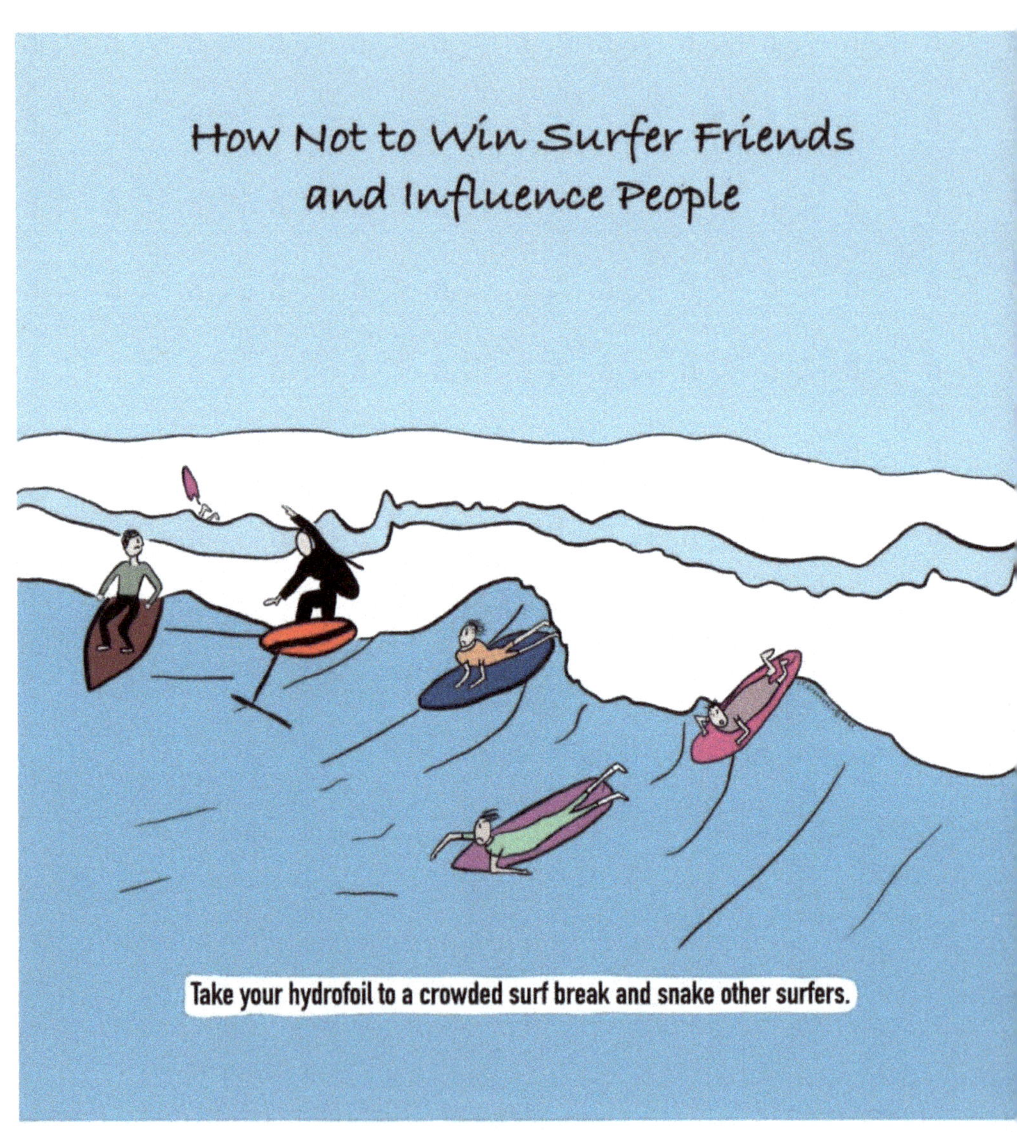

Take your hydrofoil to a crowded surf break and snake other surfers.

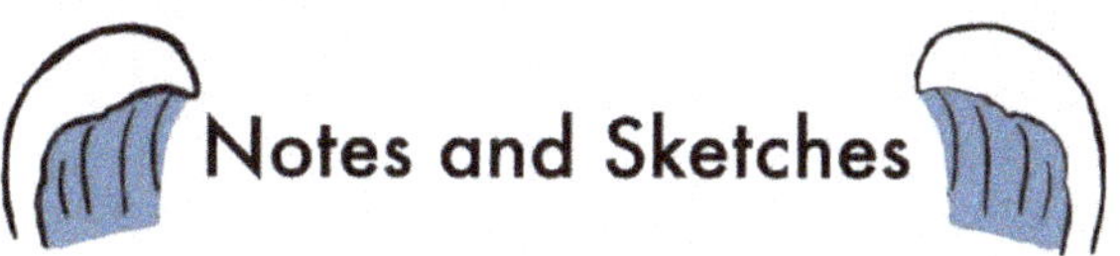

Notes and Sketches

How Not to Win Surfer Friends and Influence People

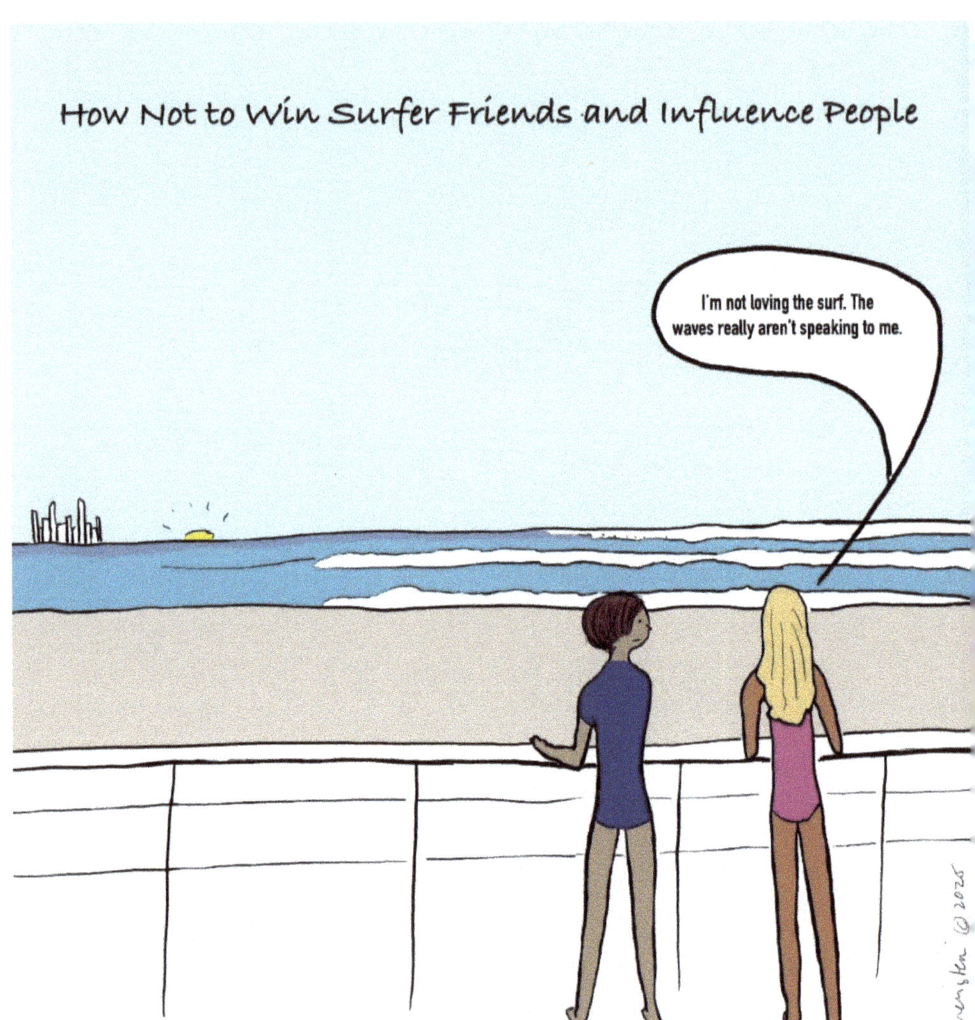

Share your lack of enthusiasm.

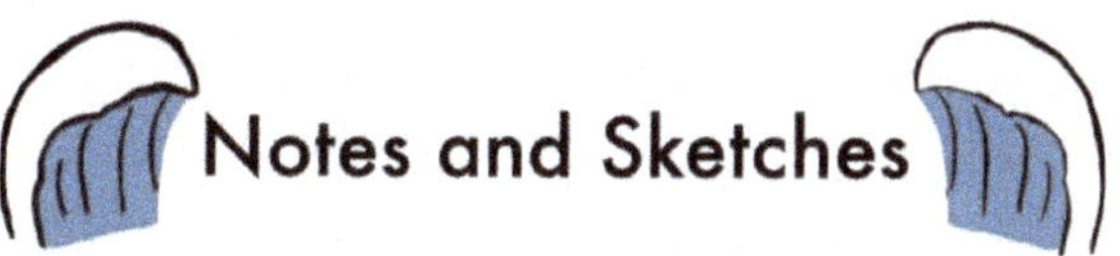

Notes and Sketches

How Not to Win Surfer Friends and Influence People

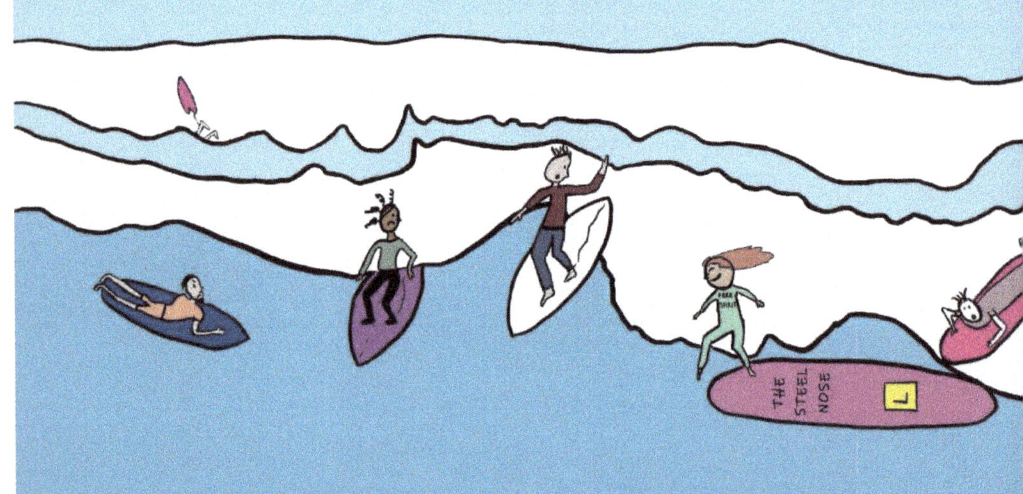

Practice your beginner – level longboarder skills at a busy surf break.
Forget your leash but go anyway.

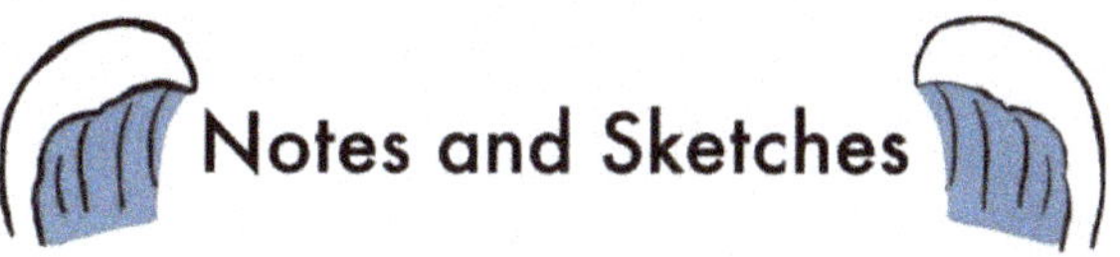

Notes and Sketches

Aquatic Creatures We Know and Love

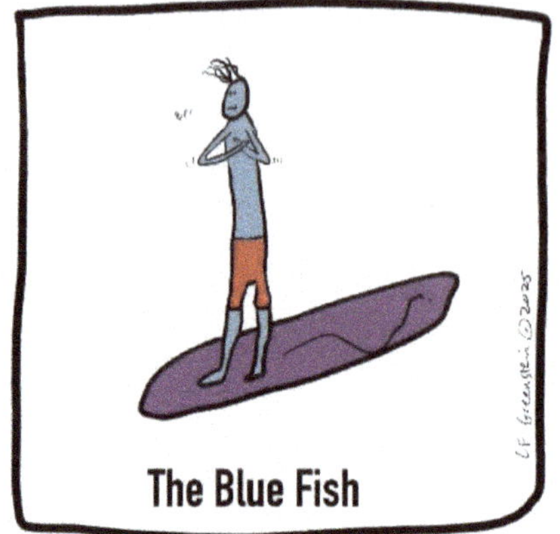

The Blue Fish

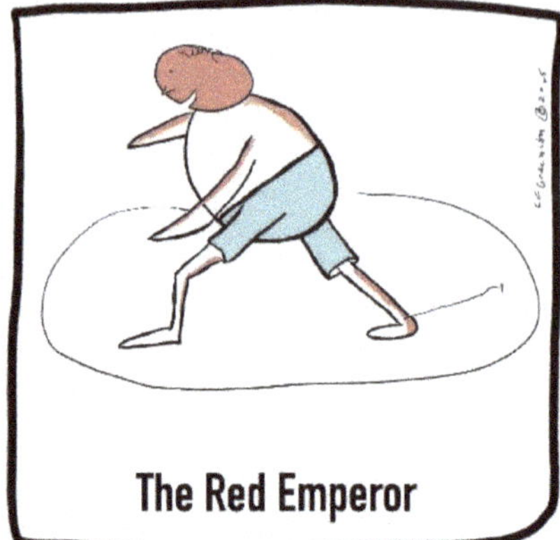

The Red Emperor

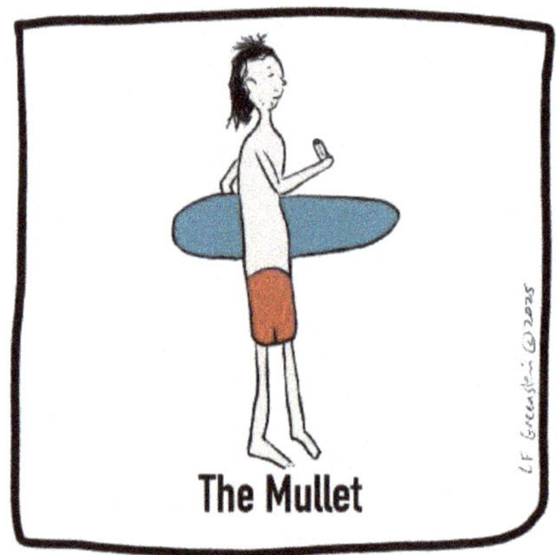

The Mullet

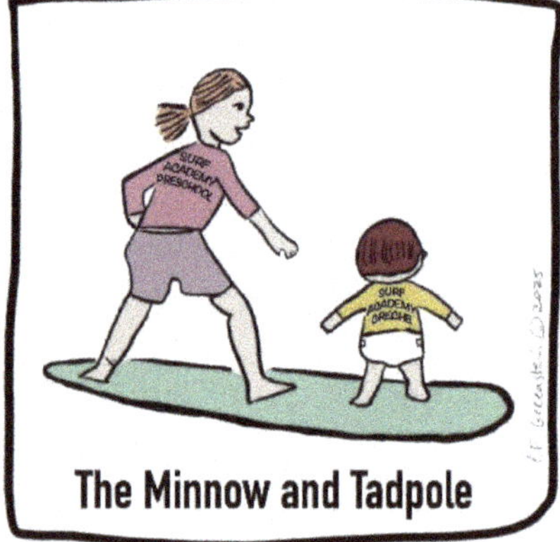

The Minnow and Tadpole

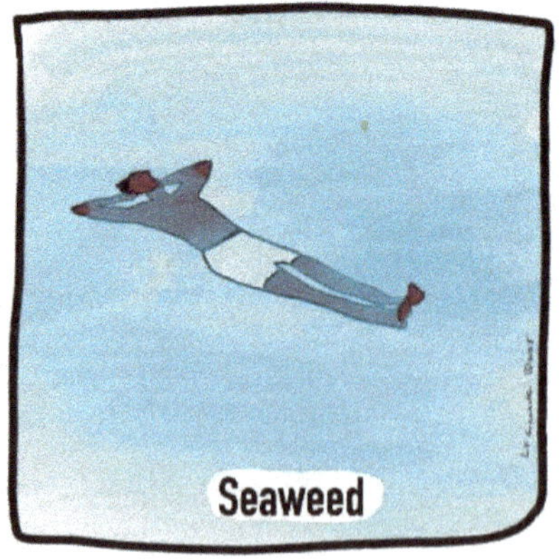

Seaweed

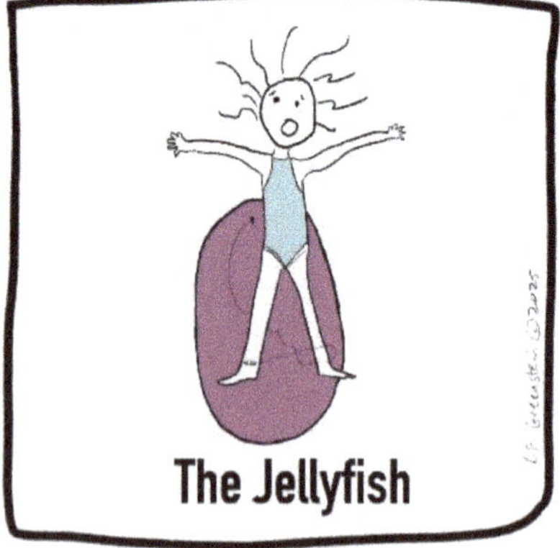

The Jellyfish

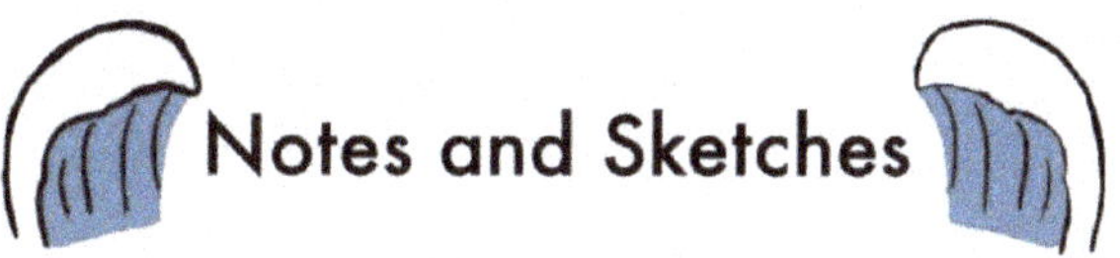

Notes and Sketches

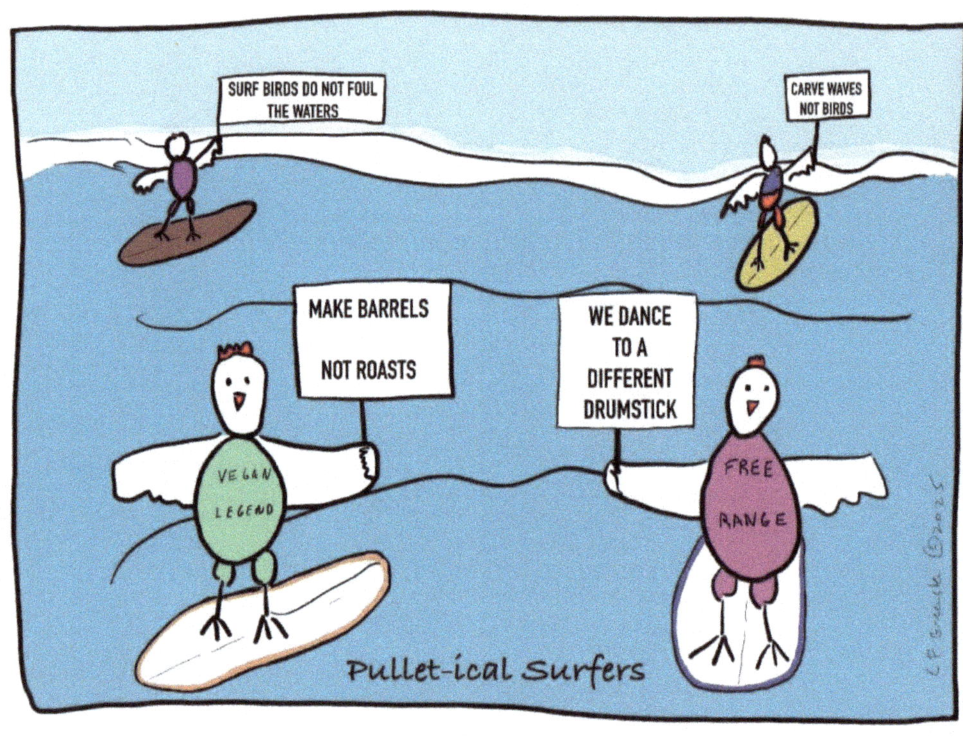

SURF BIRDS DO NOT FOUL THE WATERS
CARVE WAVES NOT BIRDS
MAKE BARRELS NOT ROASTS
WE DANCE TO A DIFFERENT DRUMSTICK
VEGAN LEGEND
FREE RANGE
Pullet-ical Surfers

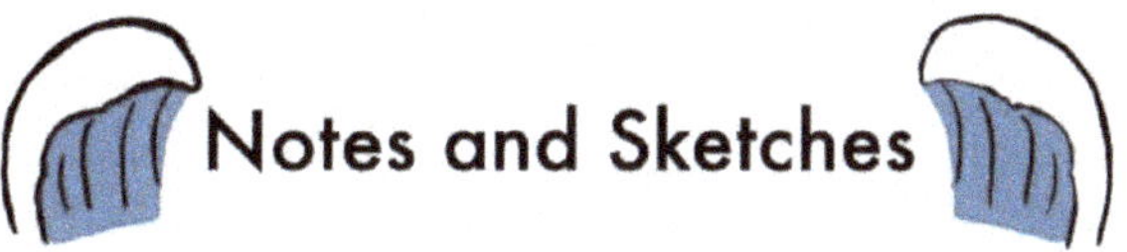

Notes and Sketches

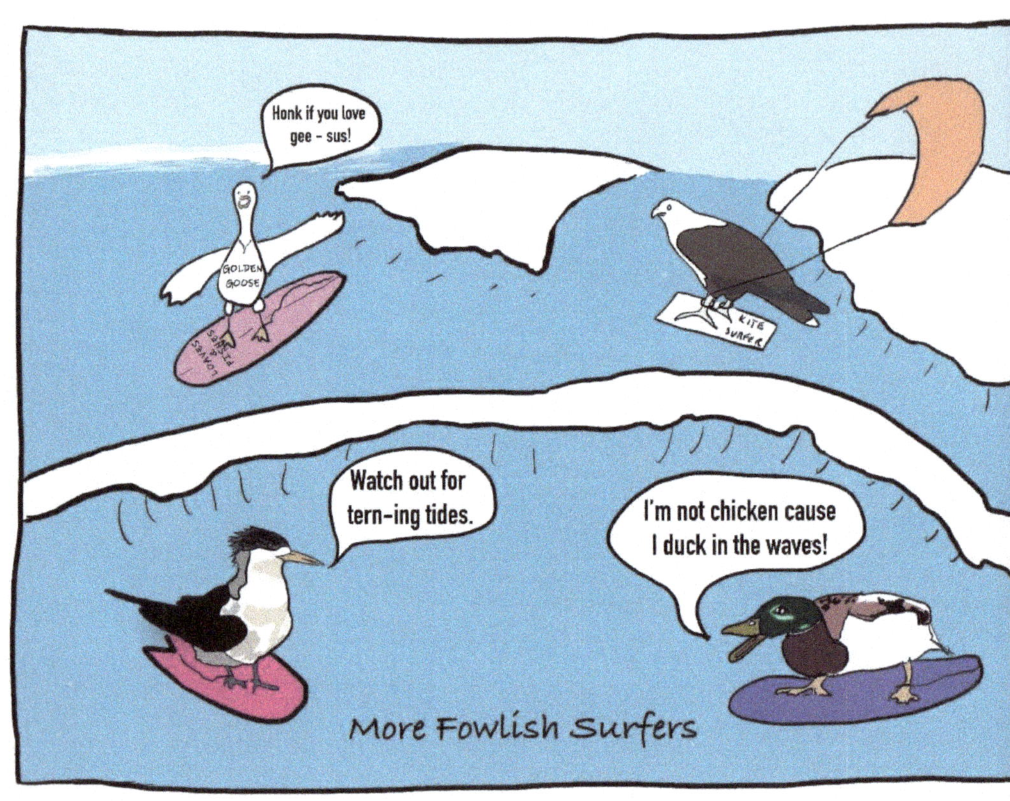

Honk if you love gee - sus!
GOLDEN GOOSE
Watch out for tern-ing tides.
I'm not chicken cause I duck in the waves!
More Fowlish Surfers

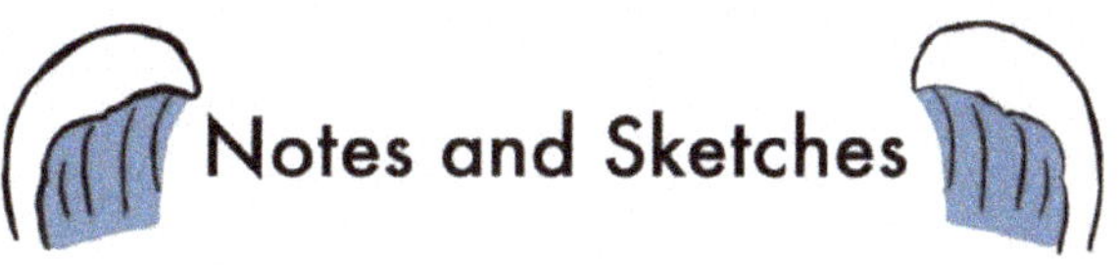

Notes and Sketches

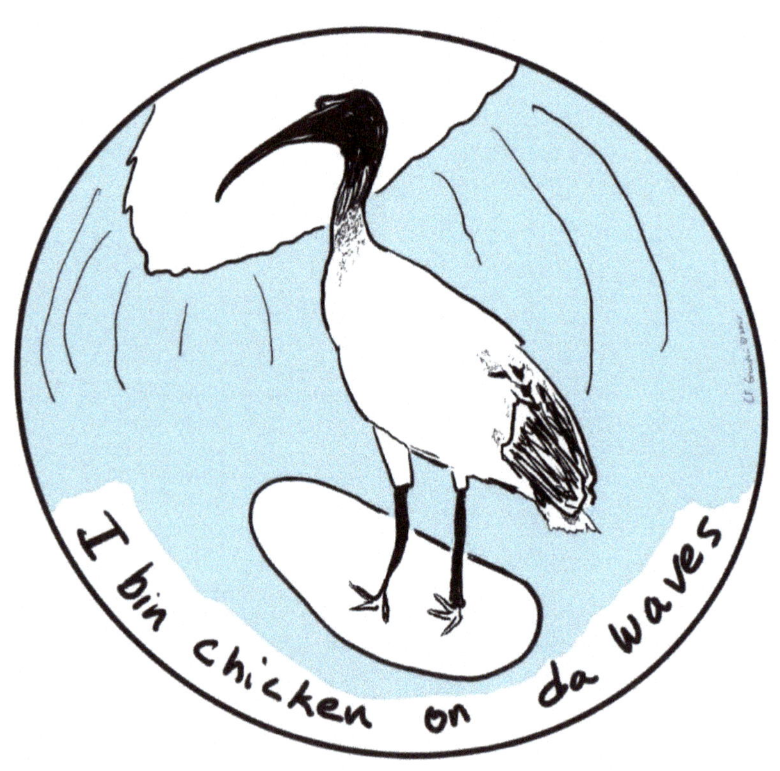

I bin chicken on da waves

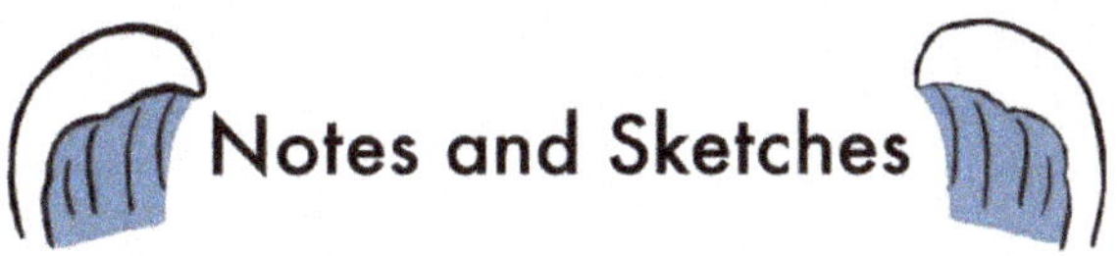

Notes and Sketches

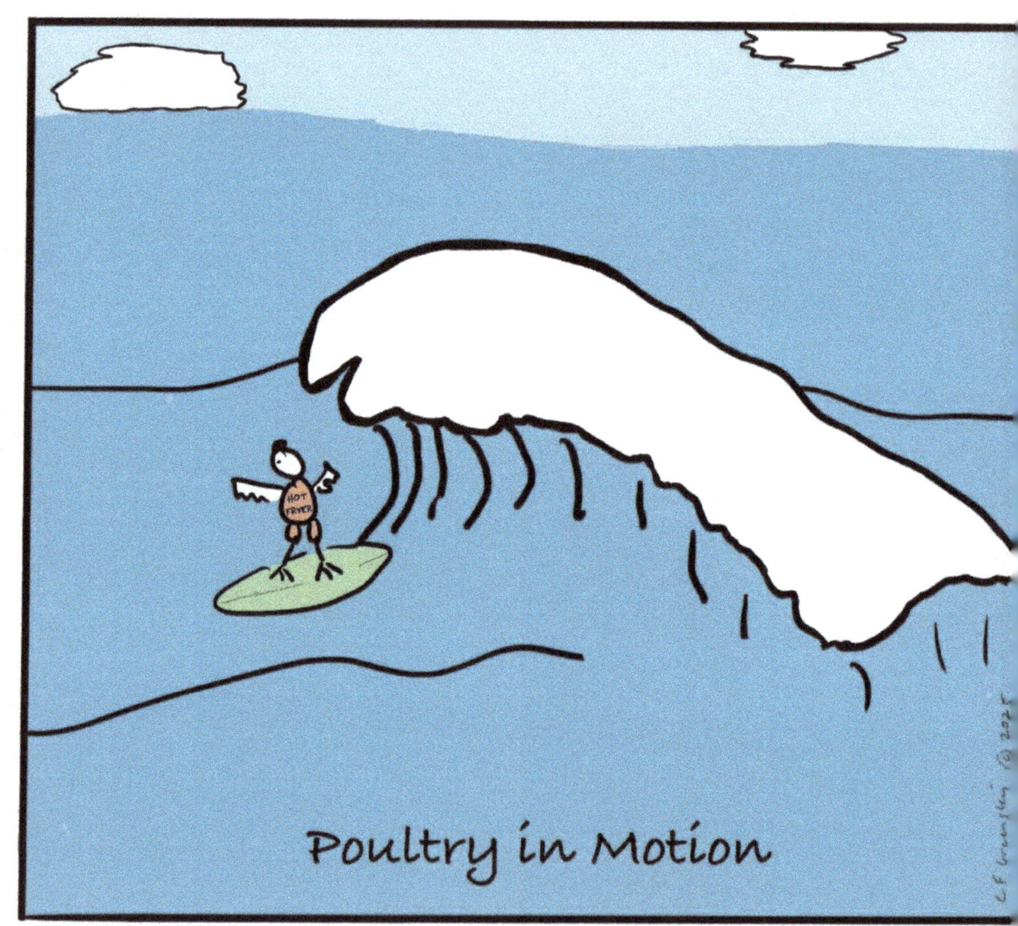

Poultry in Motion

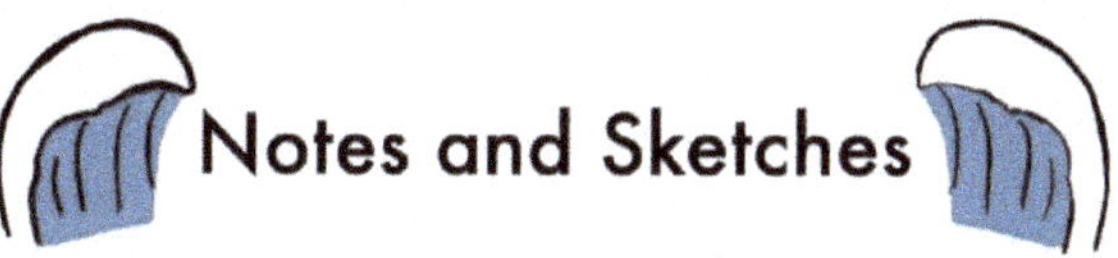

Notes and Sketches

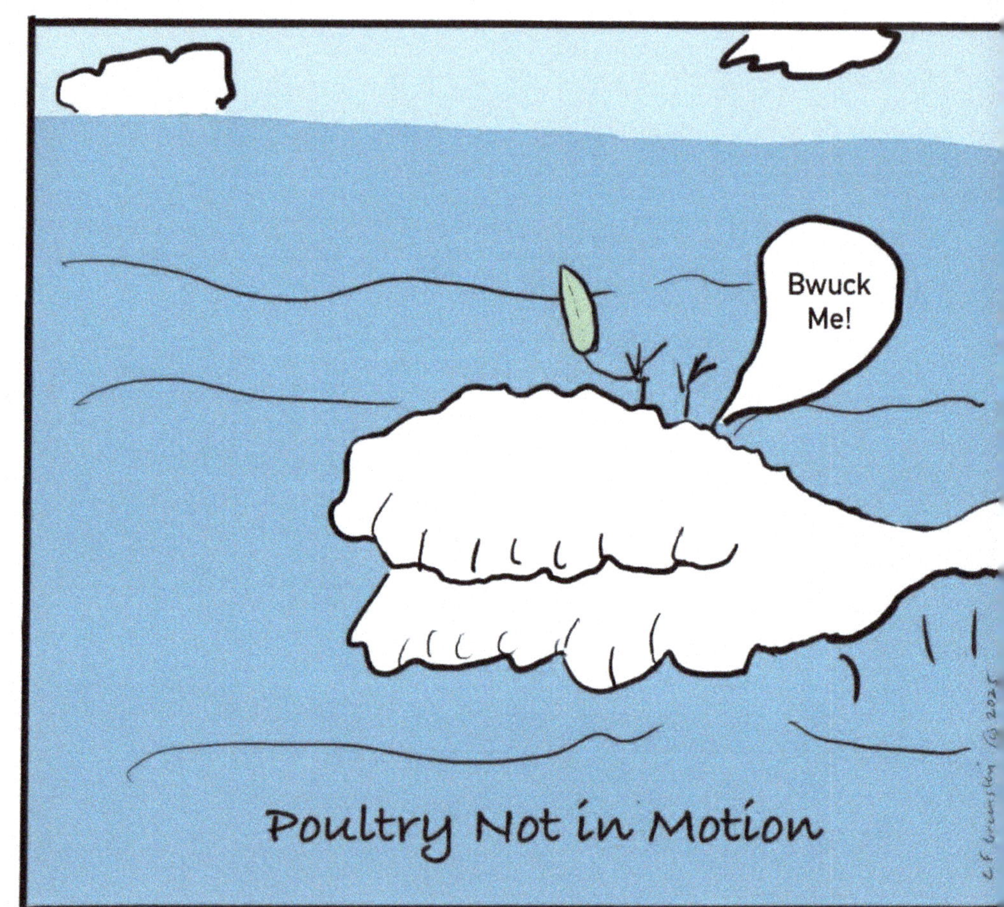

Bwuck Me!
Poultry Not in Motion

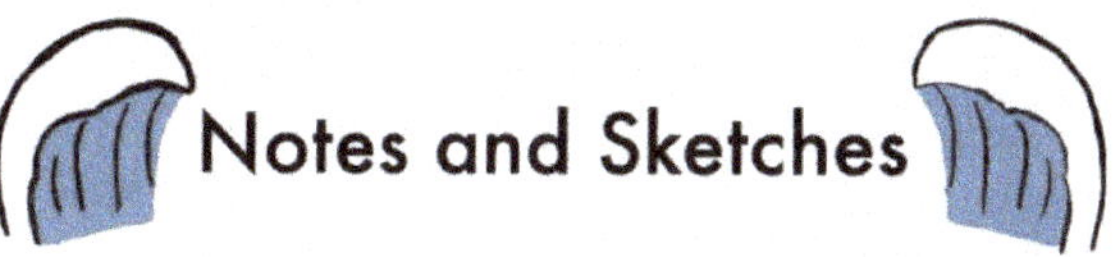

Notes and Sketches

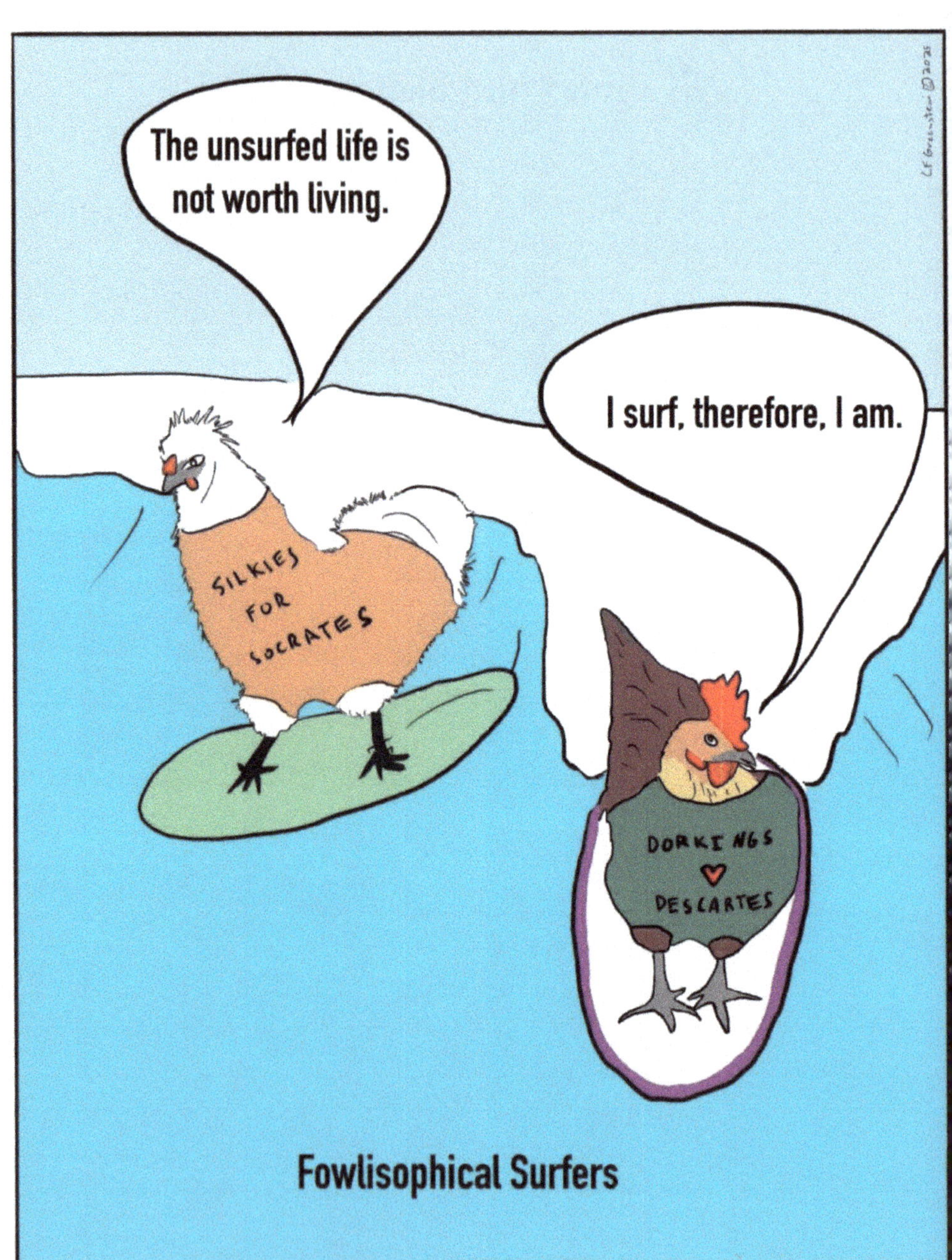

Fowlisophical Surfers

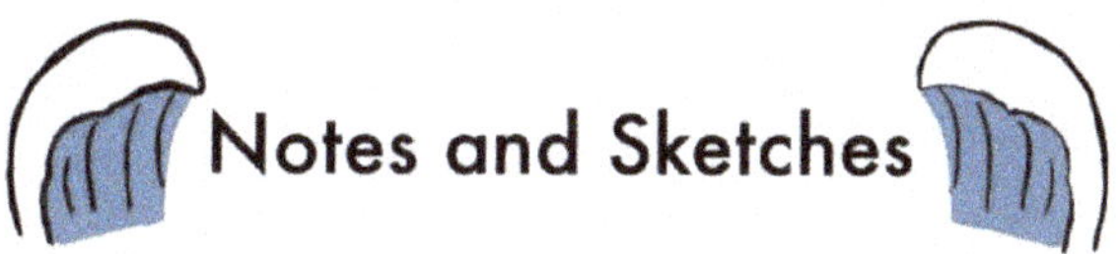
Notes and Sketches

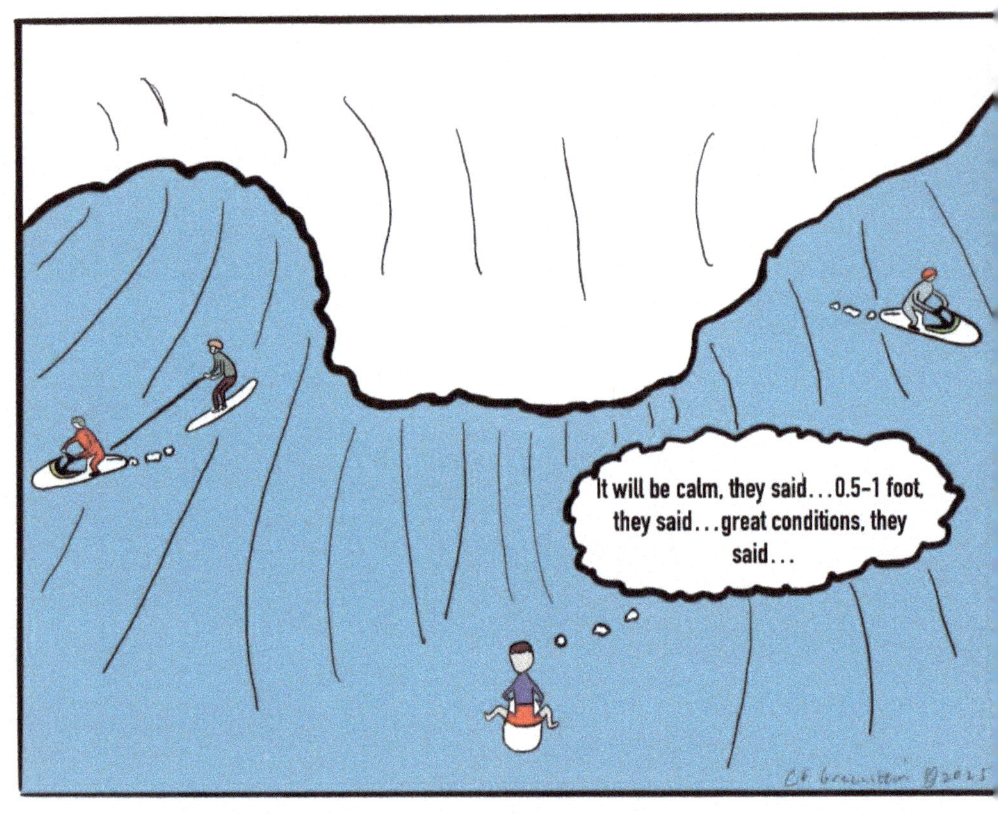

It will be calm, they said...0.5-1 foot, they said...great conditions, they said...

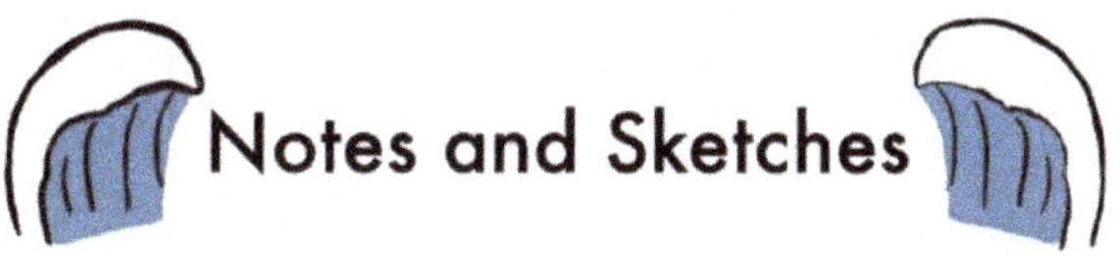
Notes and Sketches

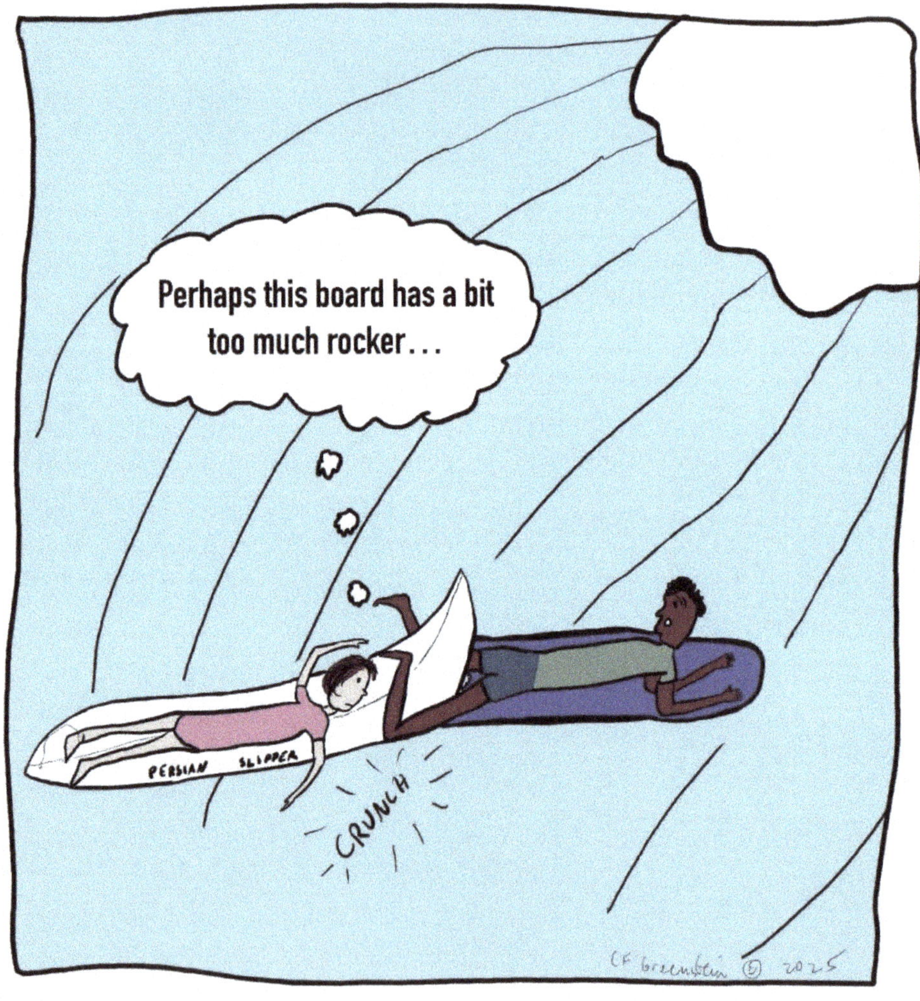

Perhaps this board has a bit too much rocker...
PERSIAN SLIPPER
CRUNCH
CF Greenstein © 2025

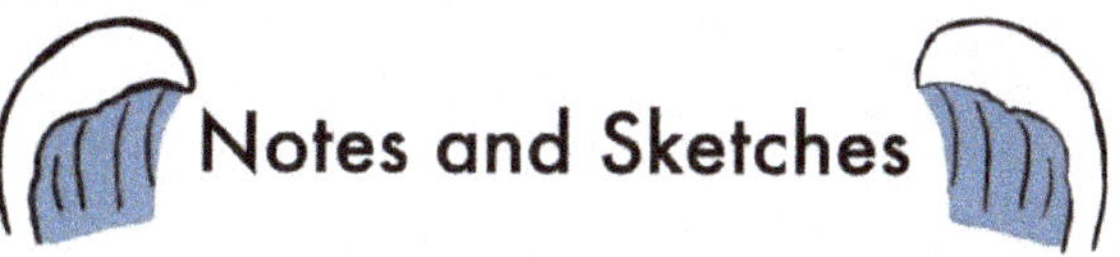
Notes and Sketches

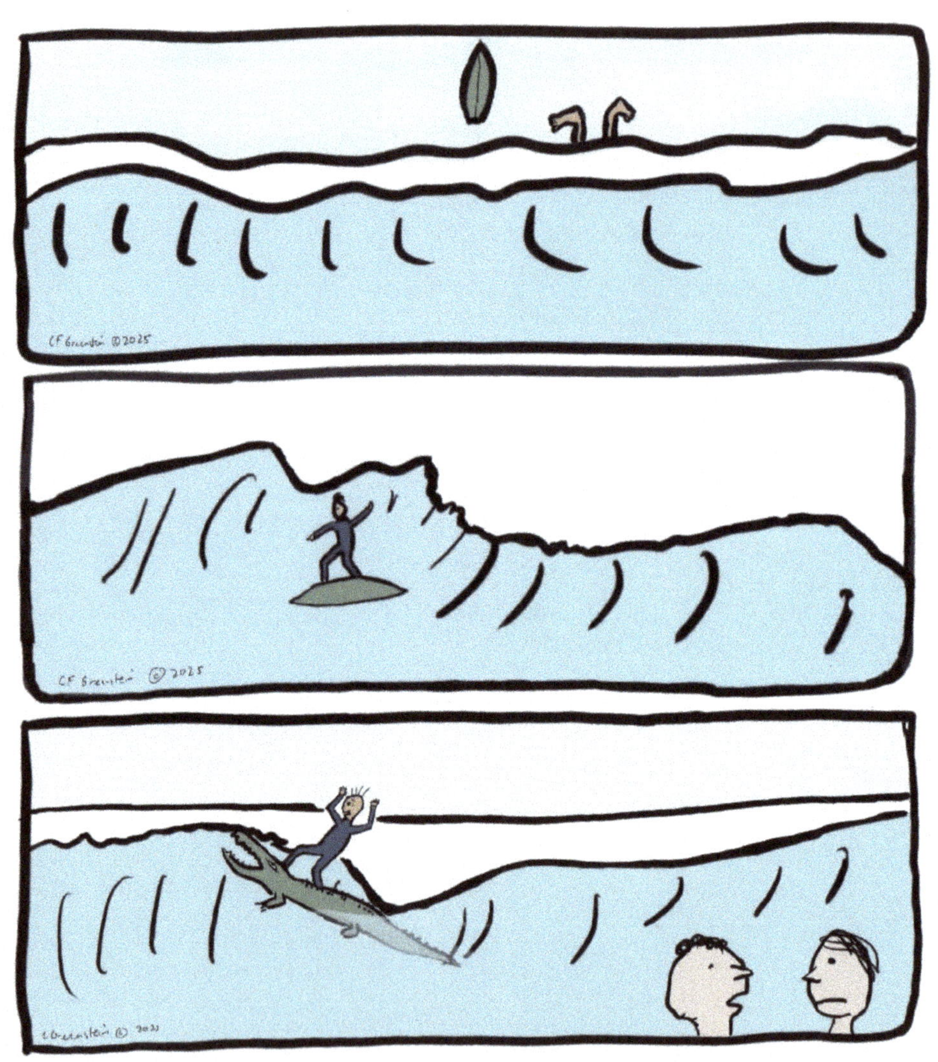

"Shoulda gone to Specsavers"

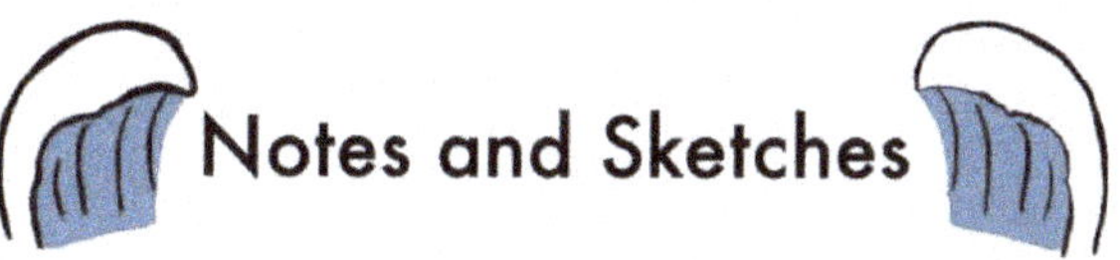

Notes and Sketches

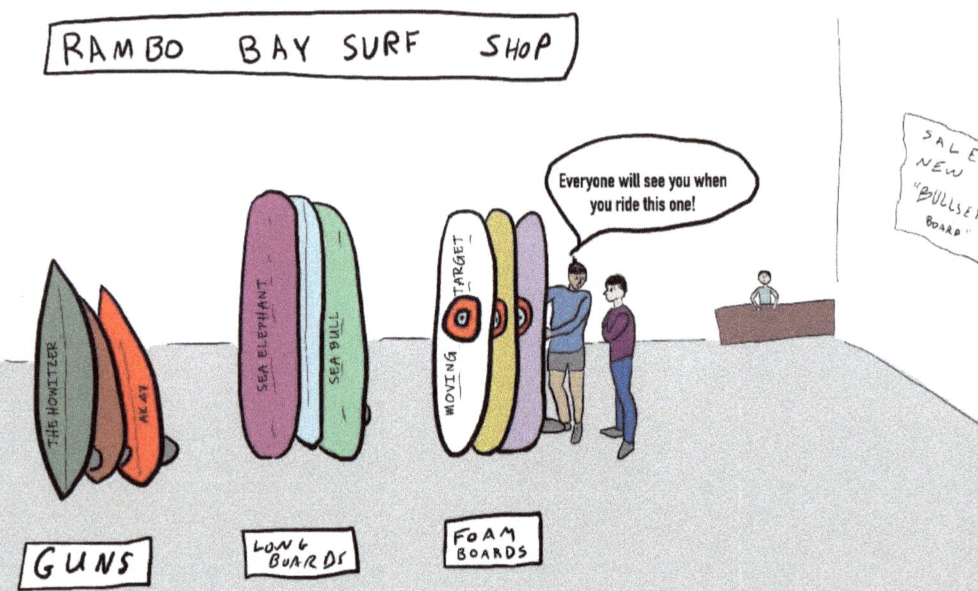

An unfortunate marketing and sales pitch.

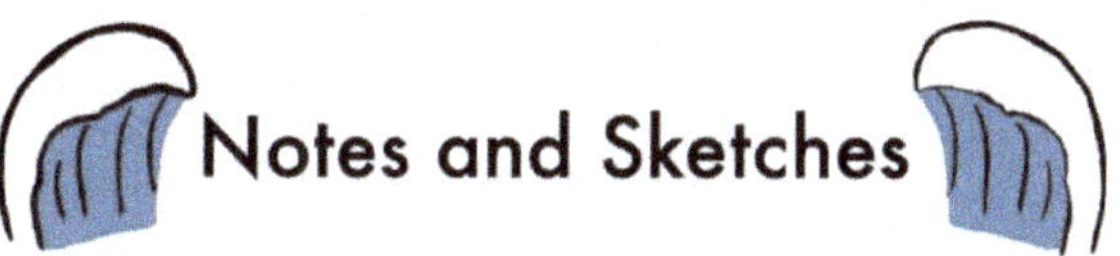

Notes and Sketches

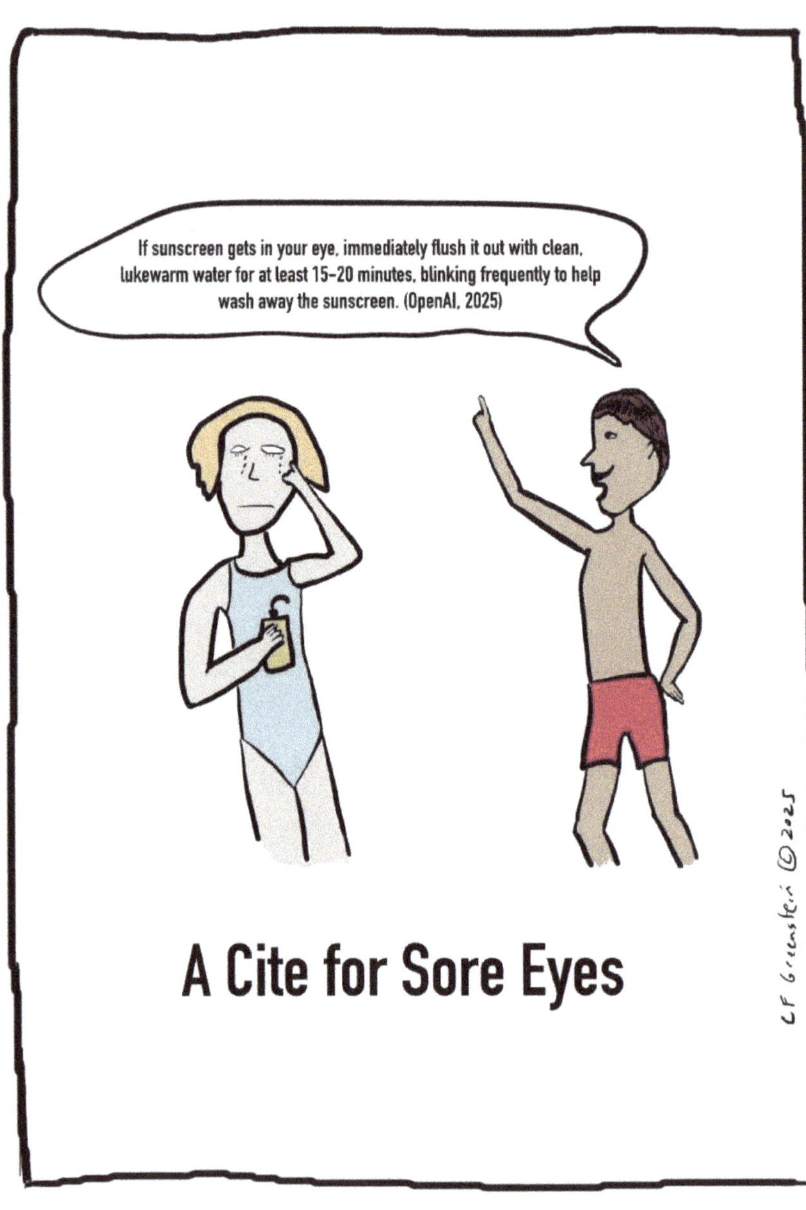

A Cite for Sore Eyes

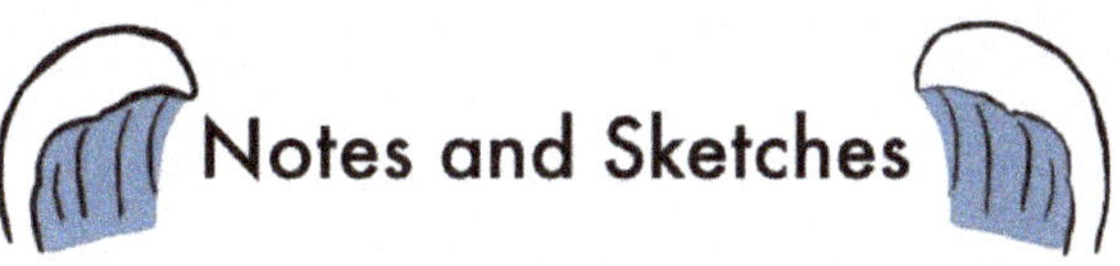

Notes and Sketches

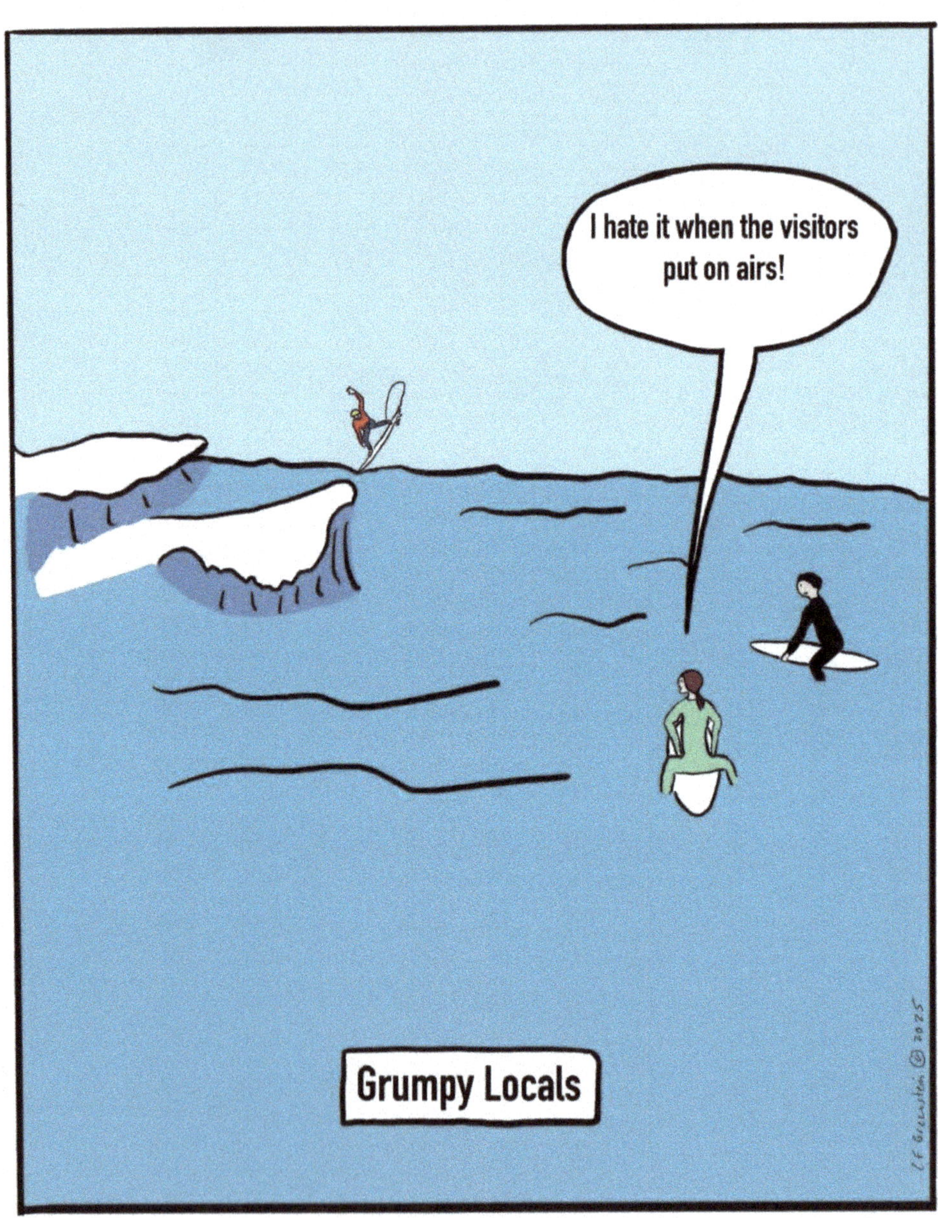

I hate it when the visitors put on airs!
Grumpy Locals

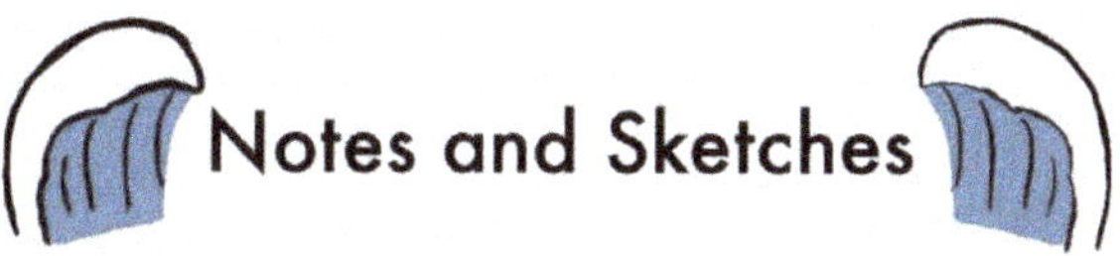

Notes and Sketches

EMBARRASSED SURFER INJURY SUPPORT GROUP

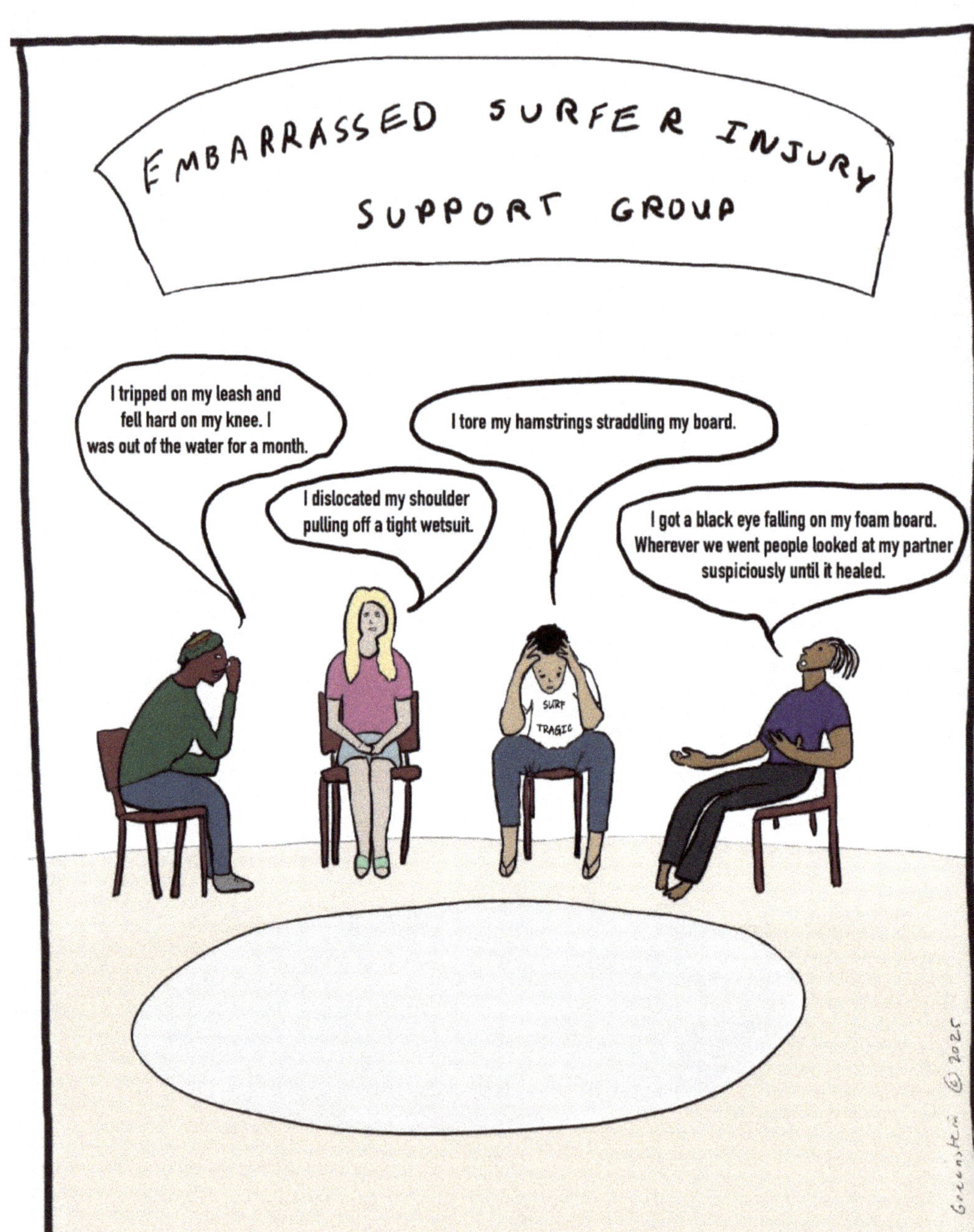

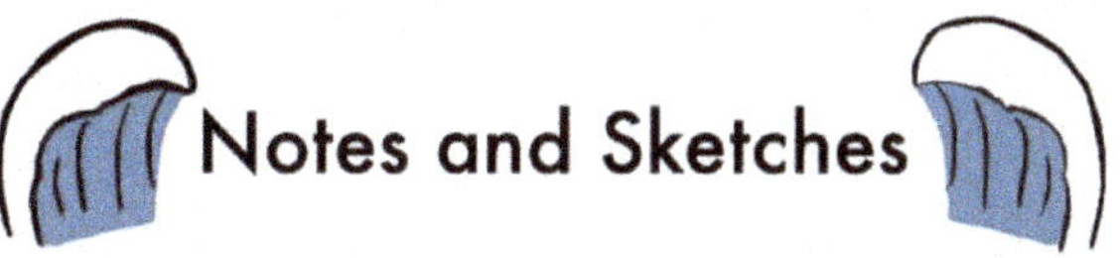

Notes and Sketches

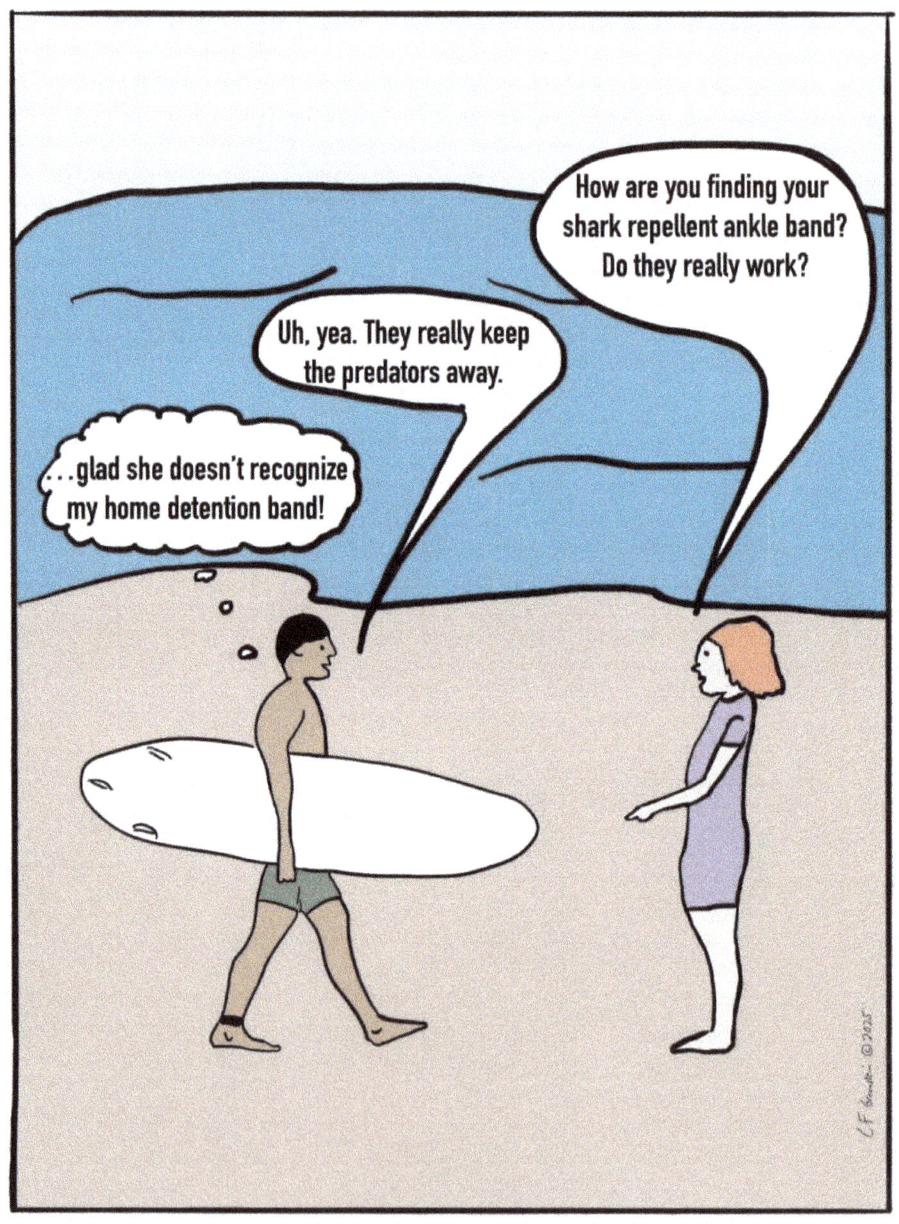

How are you finding your shark repellent ankle band? Do they really work?
Uh, yea. They really keep the predators away.
...glad she doesn't recognize my home detention band!

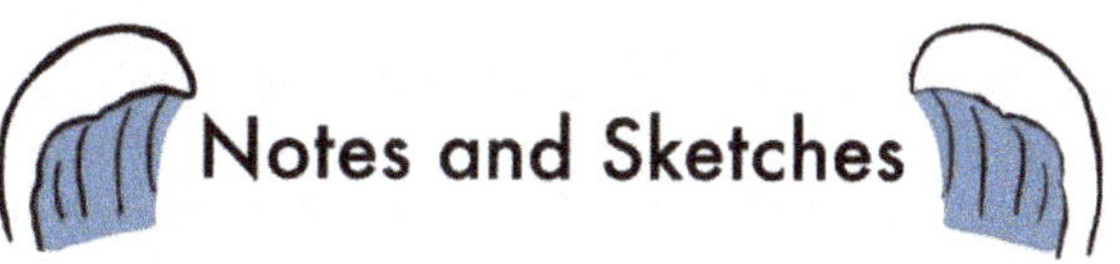

Notes and Sketches

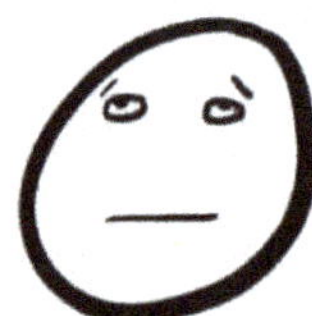

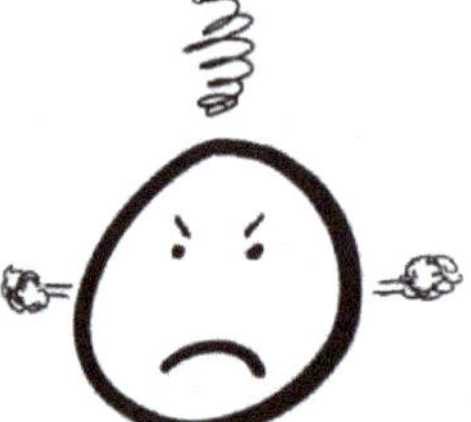
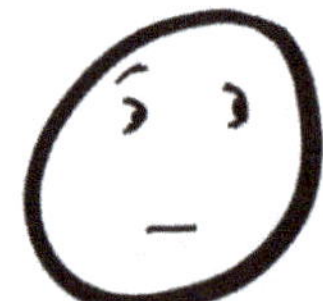

A Guide to Nonverbal Surfer Responses to
"How was your day?"
Flat Conditions
Busy surf break
Blissful
Somebody ran into me
and dinged my board.
I will tell you after my surf...
LF Greenstein © 2025

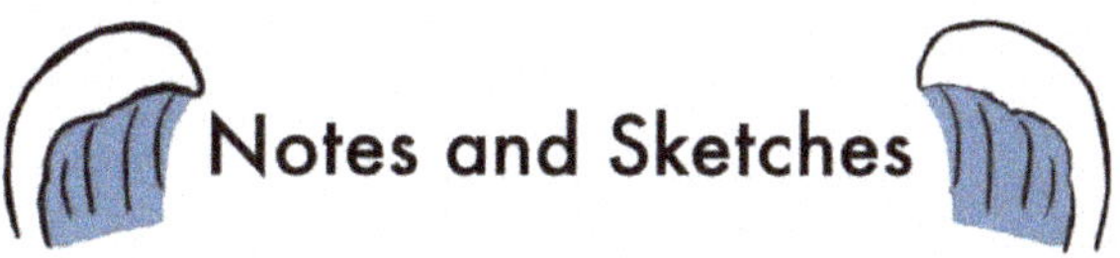

Notes and Sketches

A SHORT (BOARD) ROMANCE

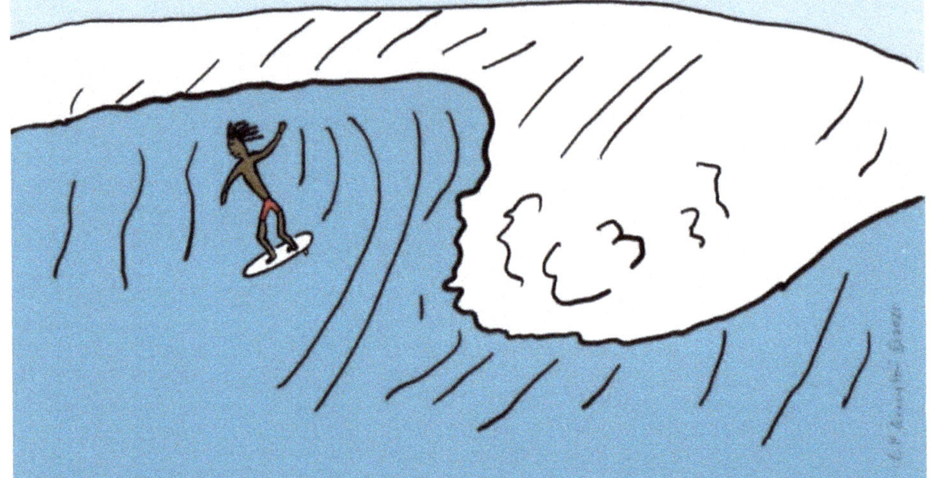

You notice his smooth paddle
and take off...

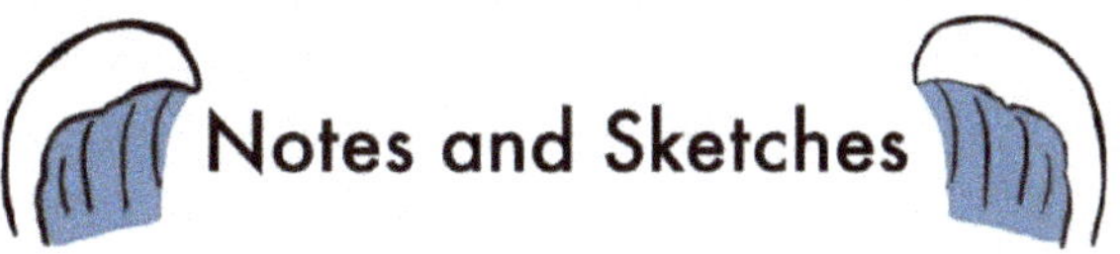

Notes and Sketches

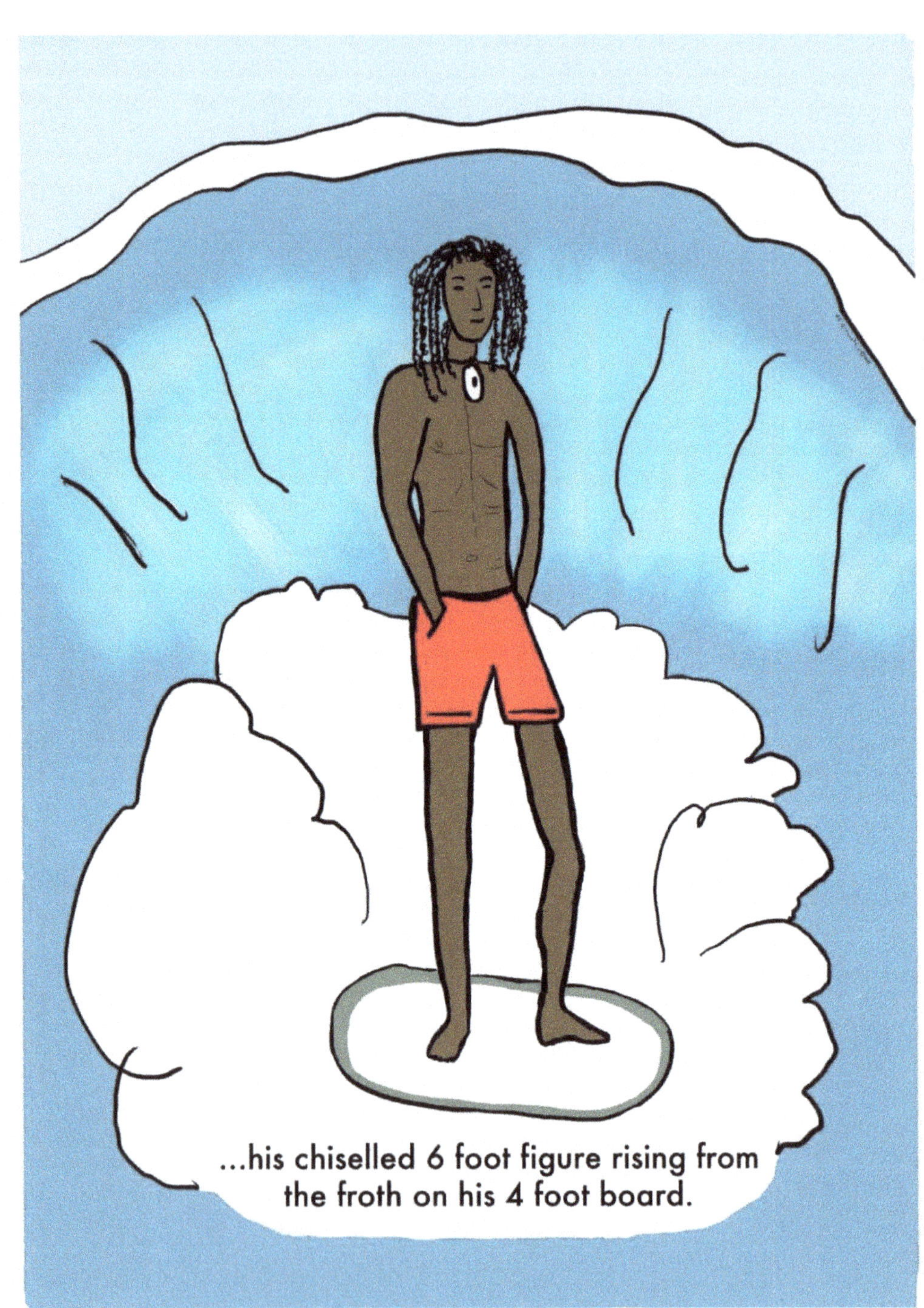

...his chiselled 6 foot figure rising from
the froth on his 4 foot board.

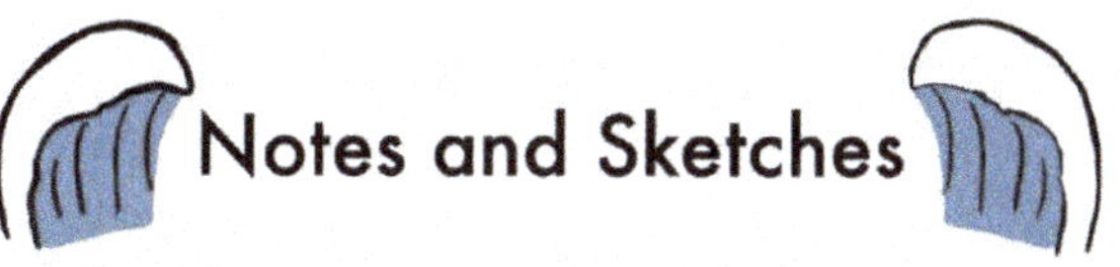

Notes and Sketches

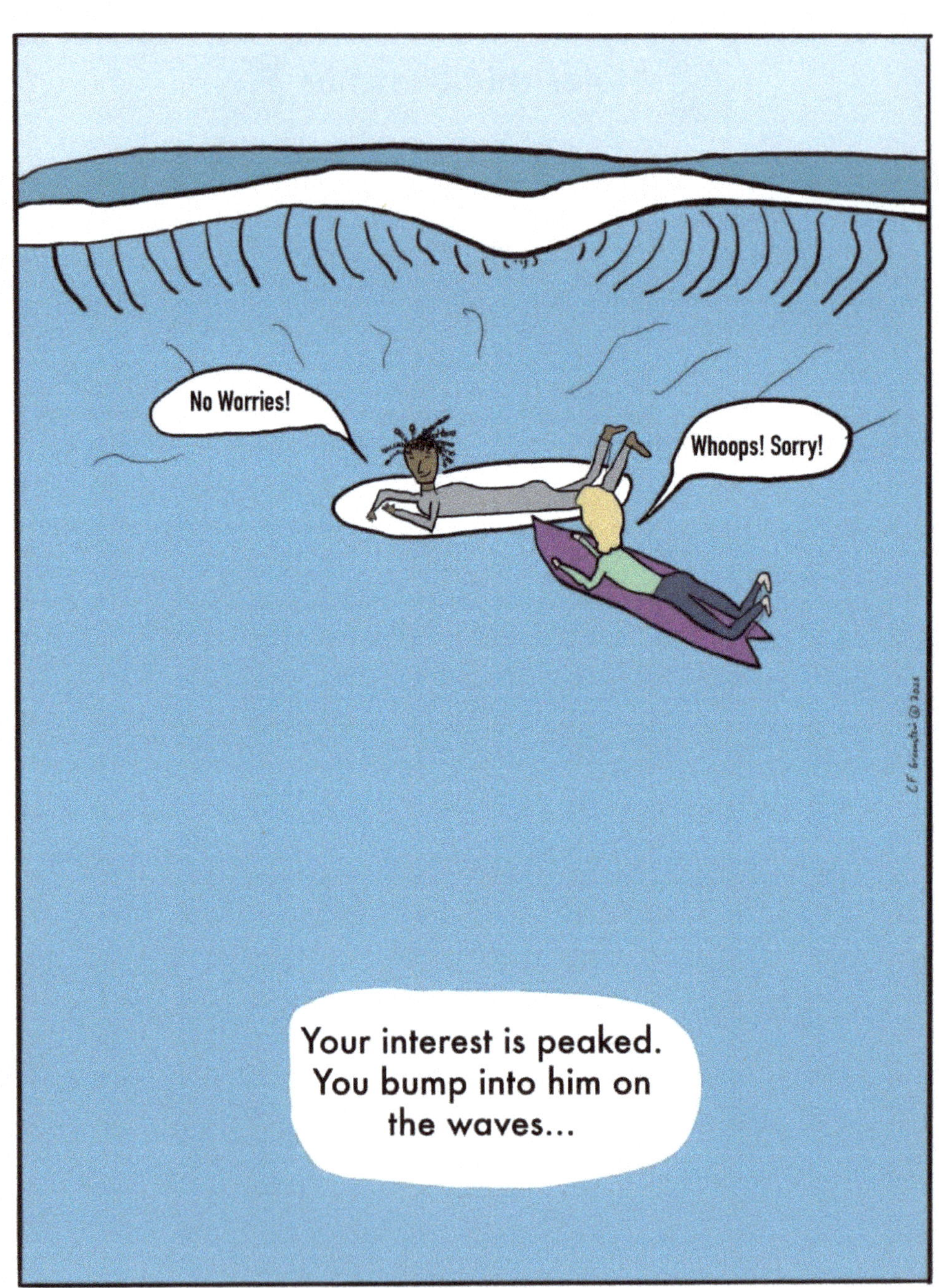

No Worries!
Whoops! Sorry!
Your interest is peaked.
You bump into him on
the waves...

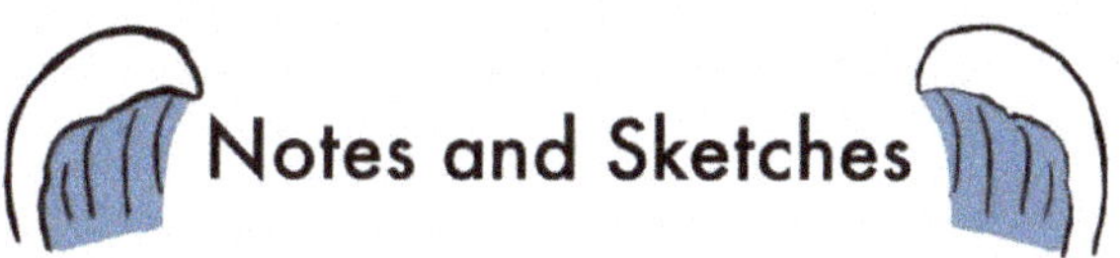

Notes and Sketches

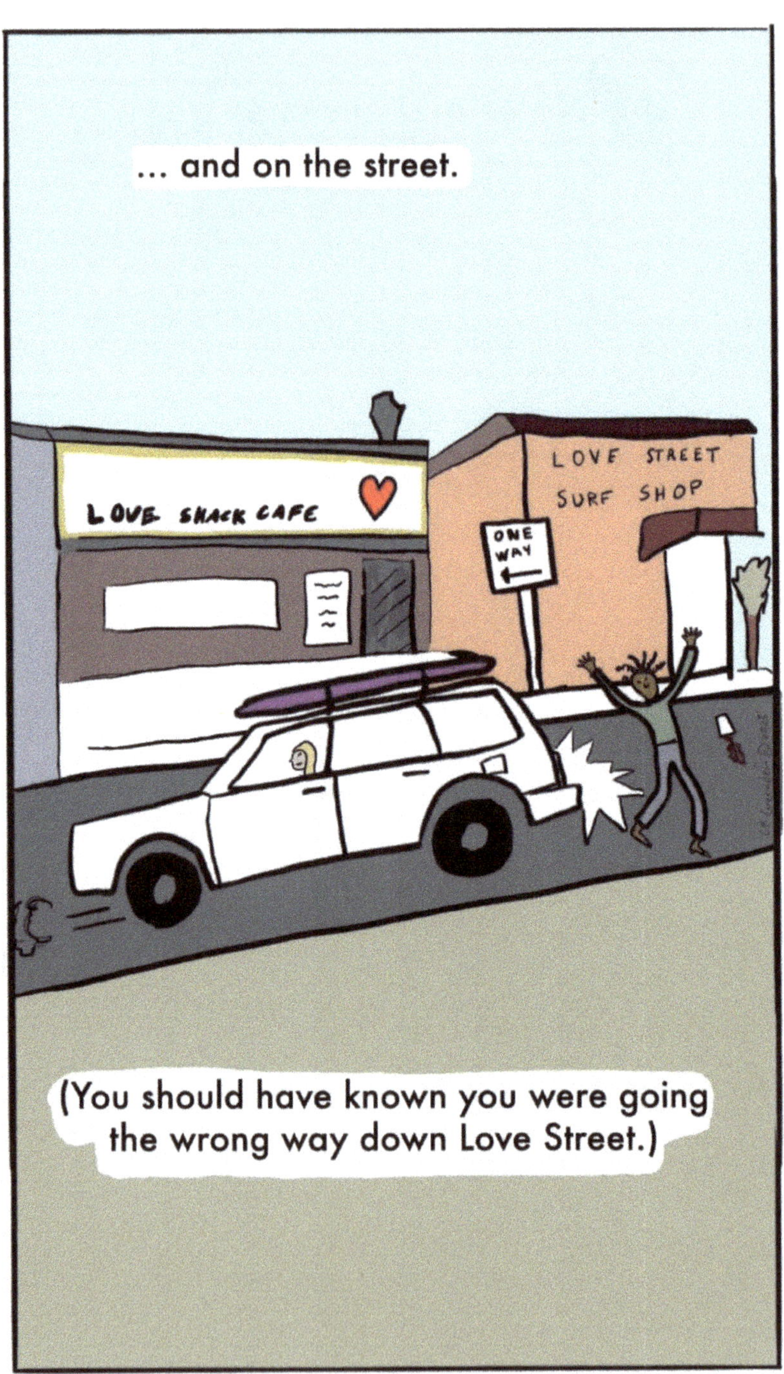
... and on the street.
LOVE SHACK CAFE
LOVE STREET SURF SHOP
ONE WAY
(You should have known you were going the wrong way down Love Street.)

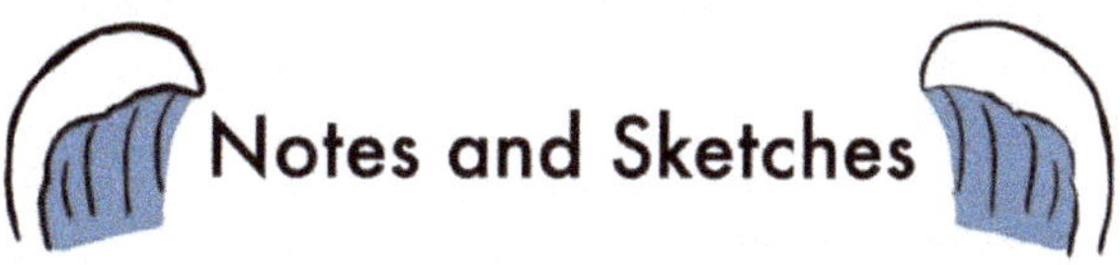

Notes and Sketches

Your eyes are like the blue of the Pacific Ocean,

Your laugh is like the roar of the waves at Teahu'po,

Your hair shines like a ray of sunlight over Jeffreys Bay…

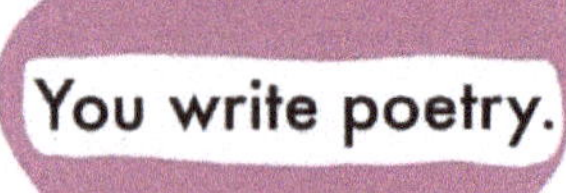

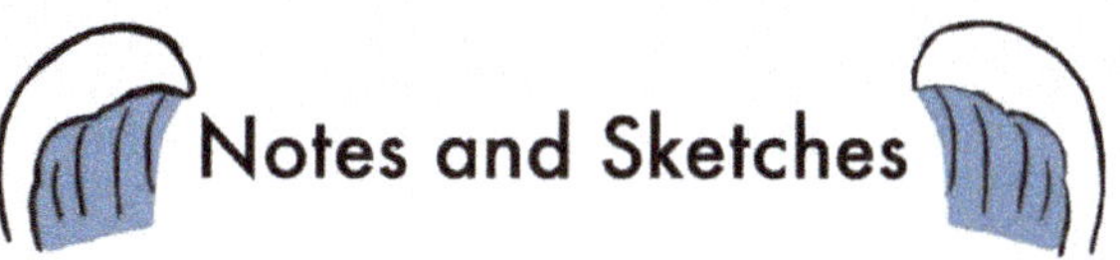

Notes and Sketches

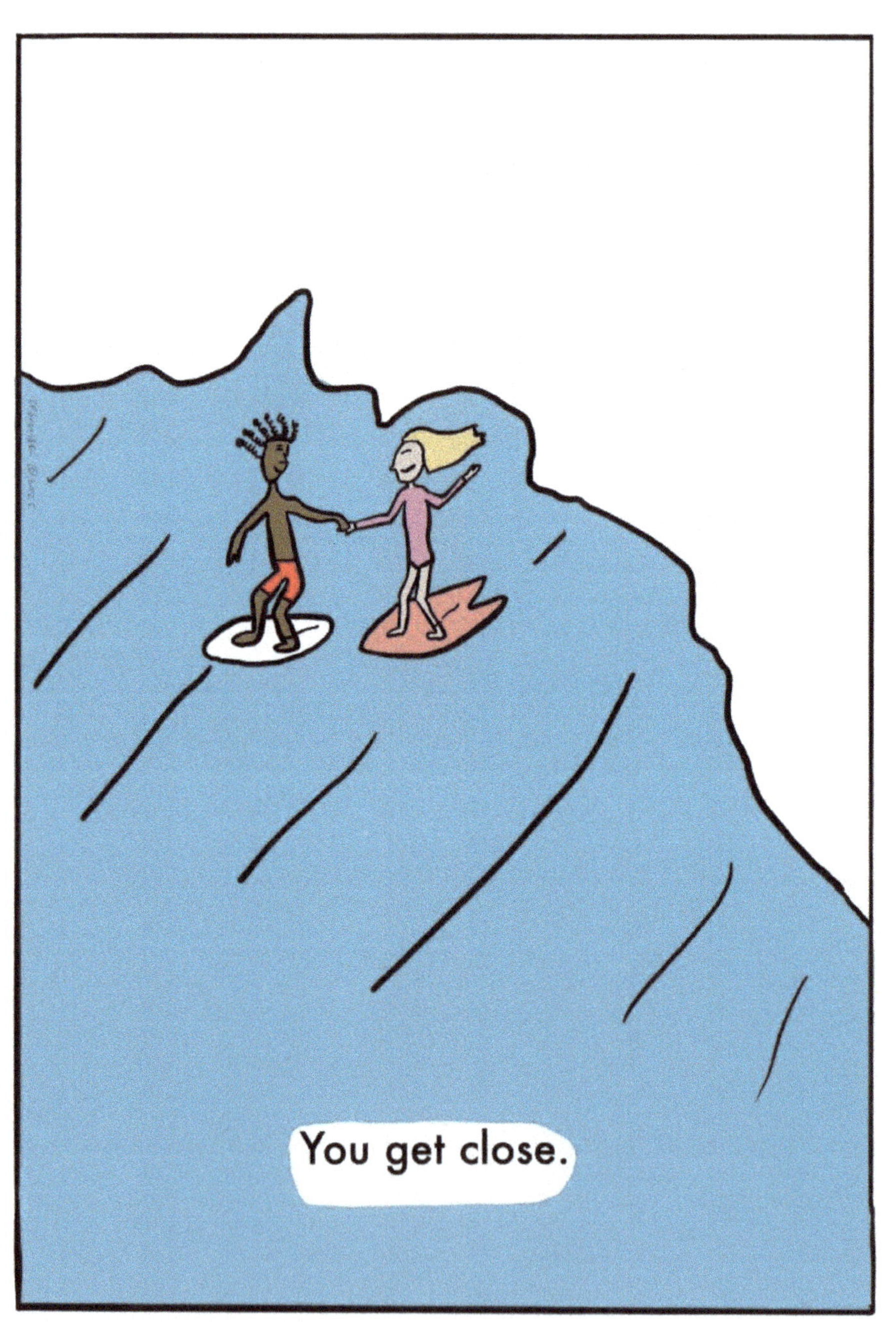
You get close.

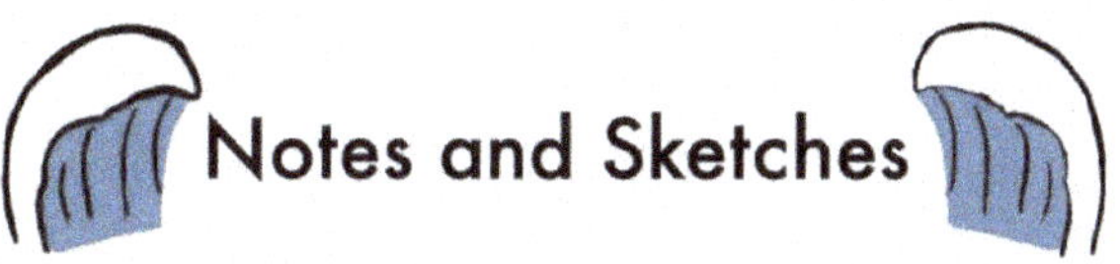

Notes and Sketches

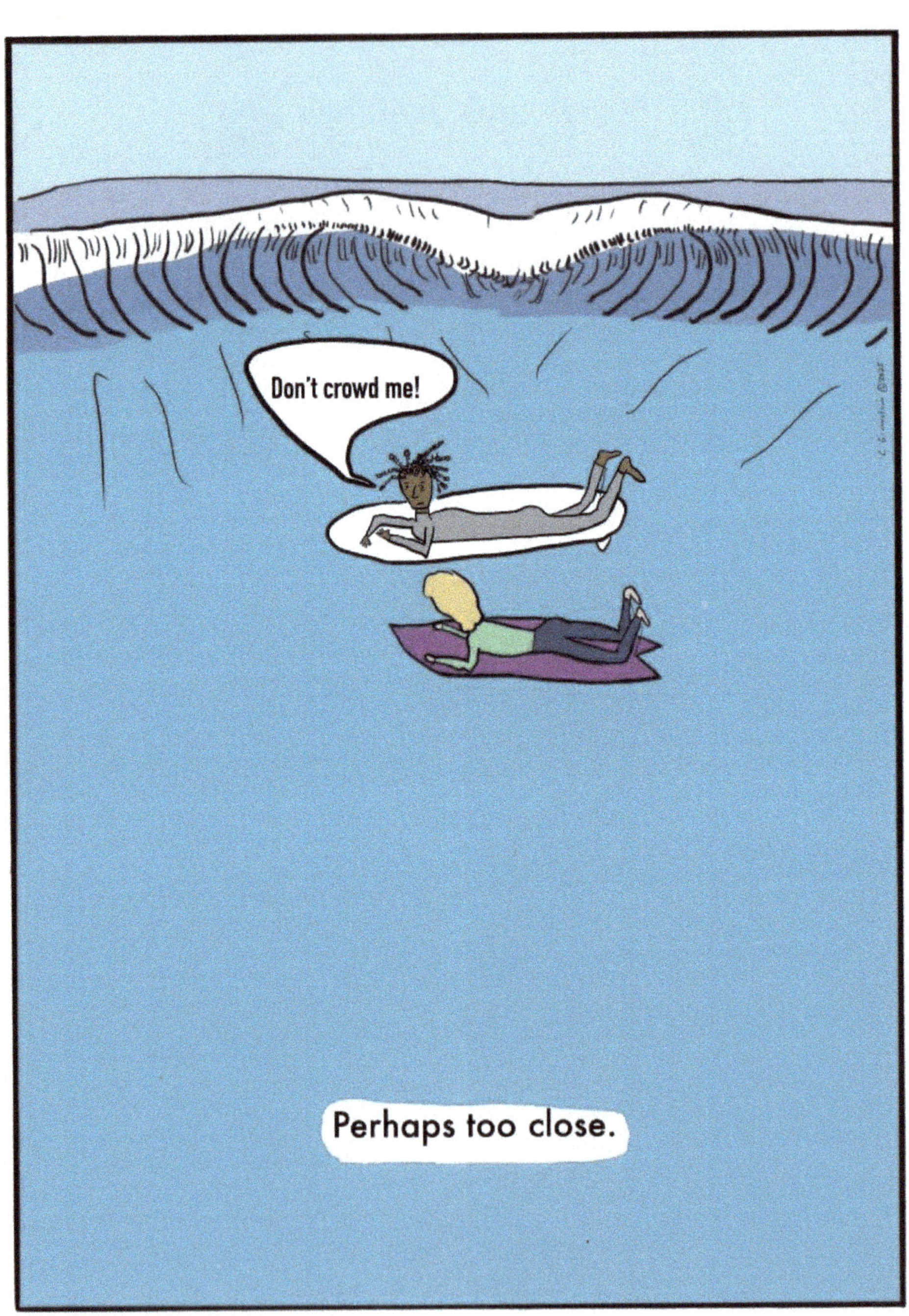

Perhaps too close.

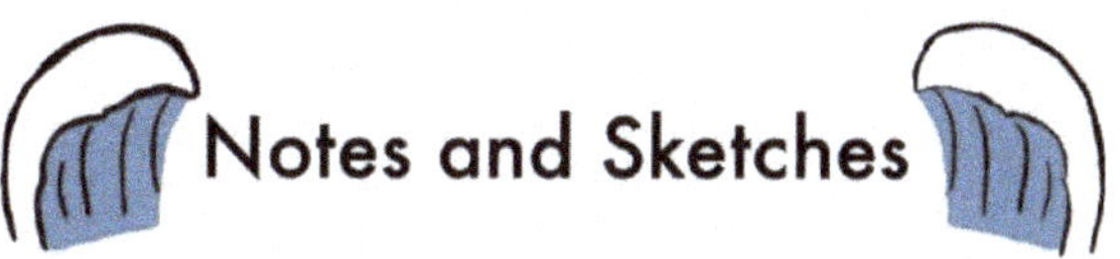

Notes and Sketches

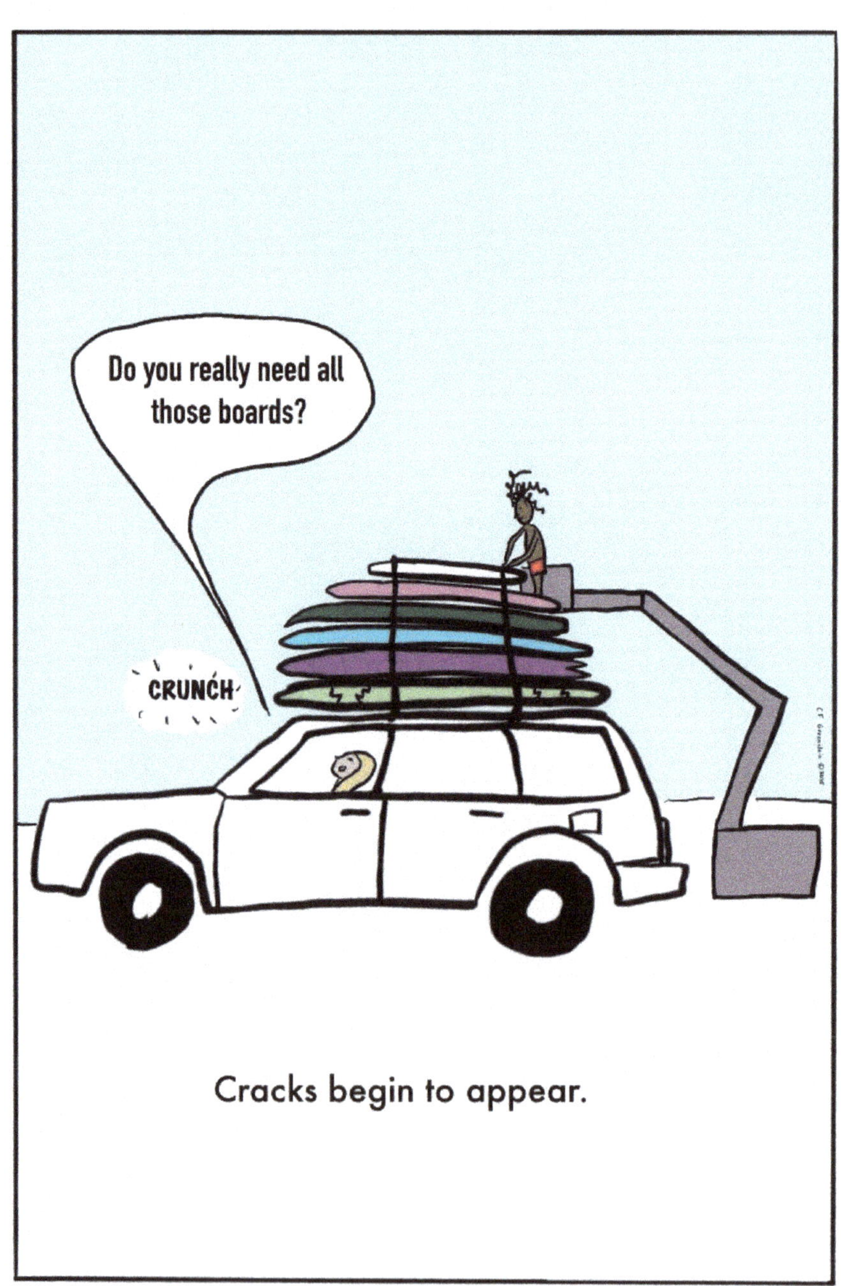

Cracks begin to appear.

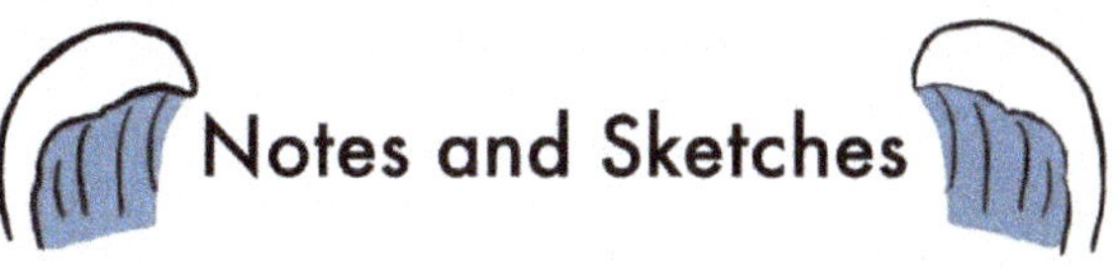

Notes and Sketches

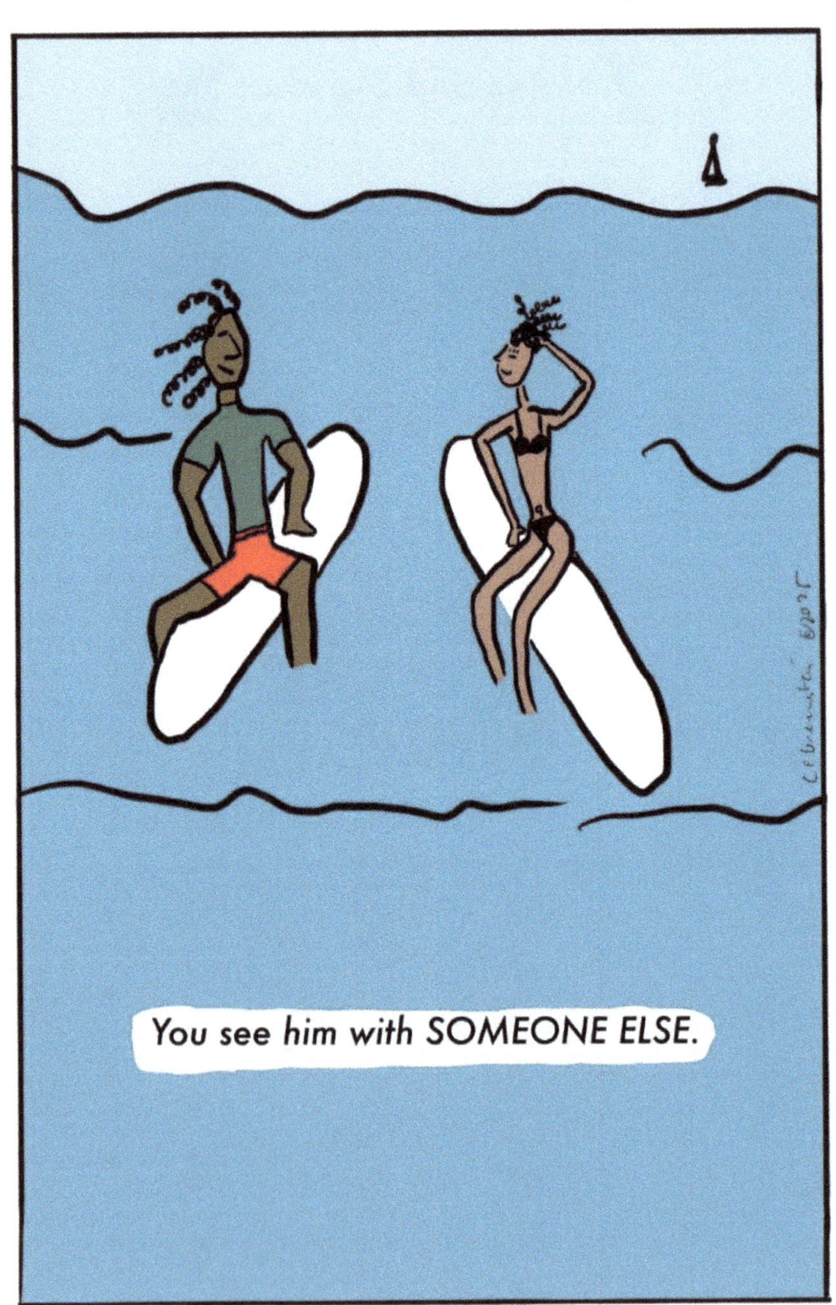

You see him with SOMEONE ELSE.

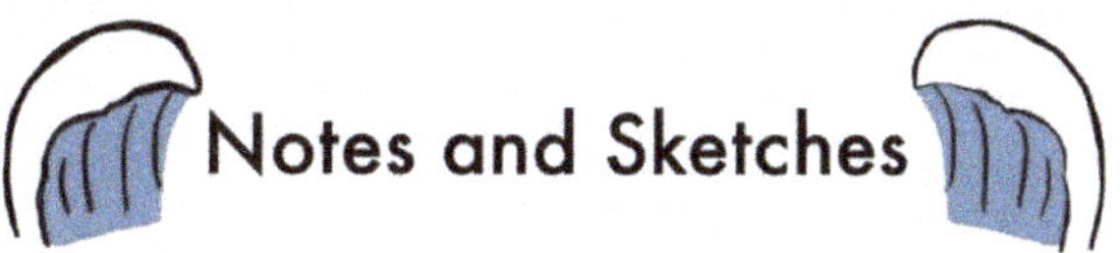

Notes and Sketches

 **tinderbox**

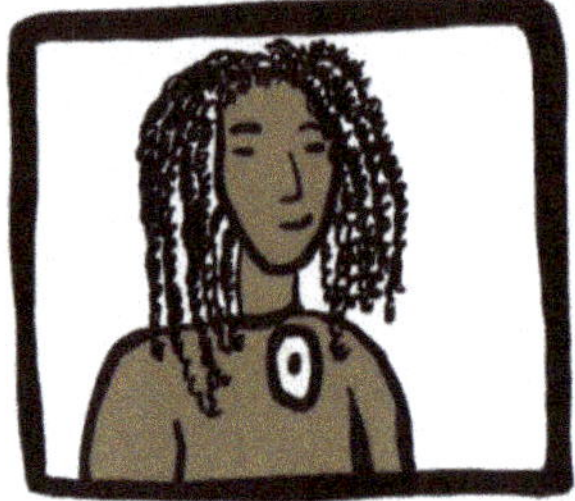

Looking for a soulmate who:

-loves (very) early morning walks

-sand between the sheets

-spending quality time together at your place (located across from surf break)

He is spotted on dating apps.

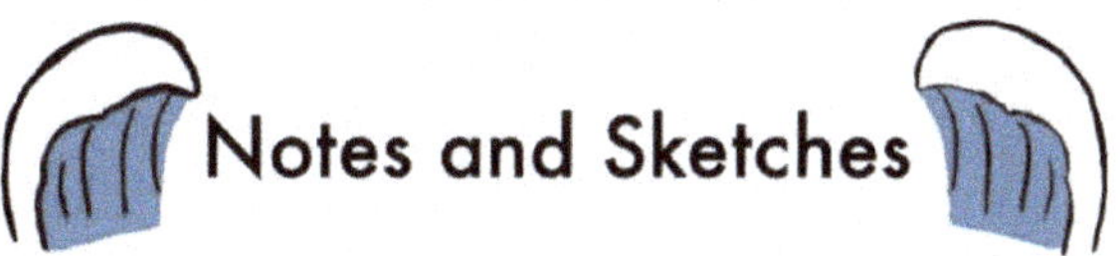

Notes and Sketches

Your eyes are like the red of a stoner's,

Your hair is like a mat of dead seaweed,

Your laugh is like the cackle of a seagull's angry call...

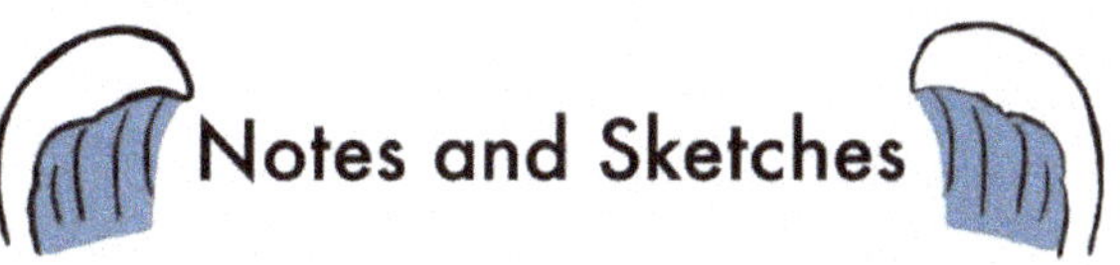

Notes and Sketches

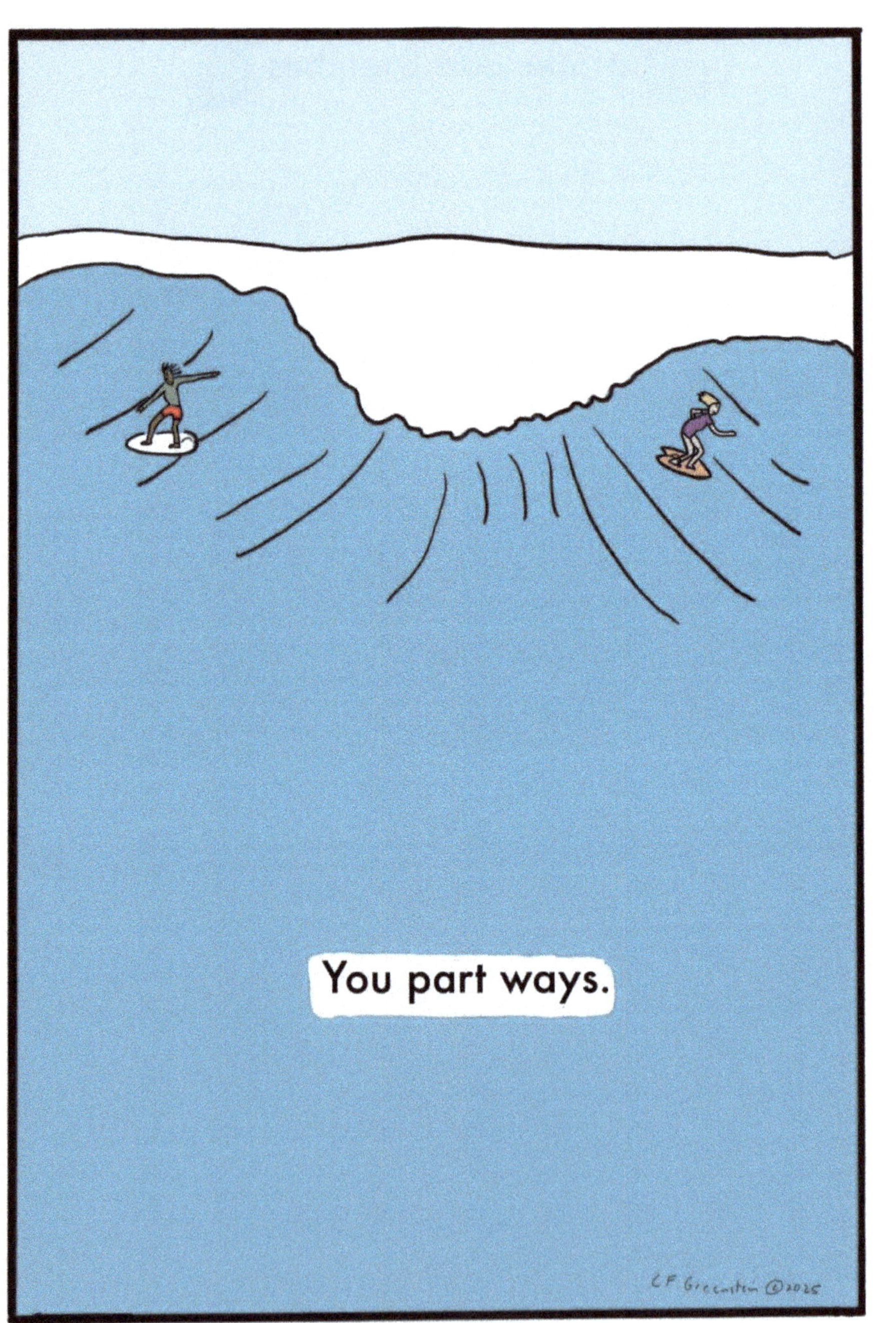

You part ways.

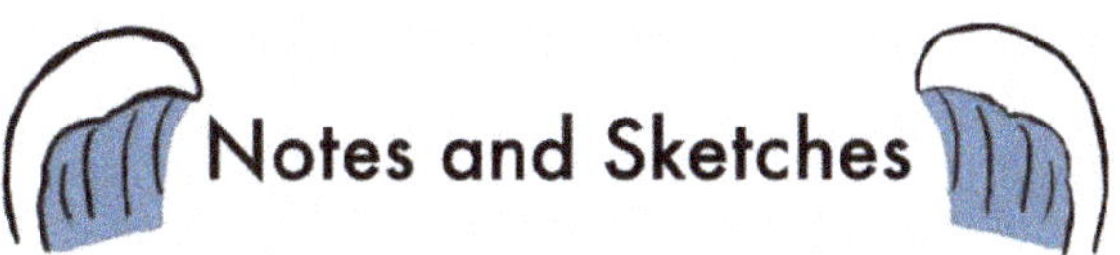

Notes and Sketches

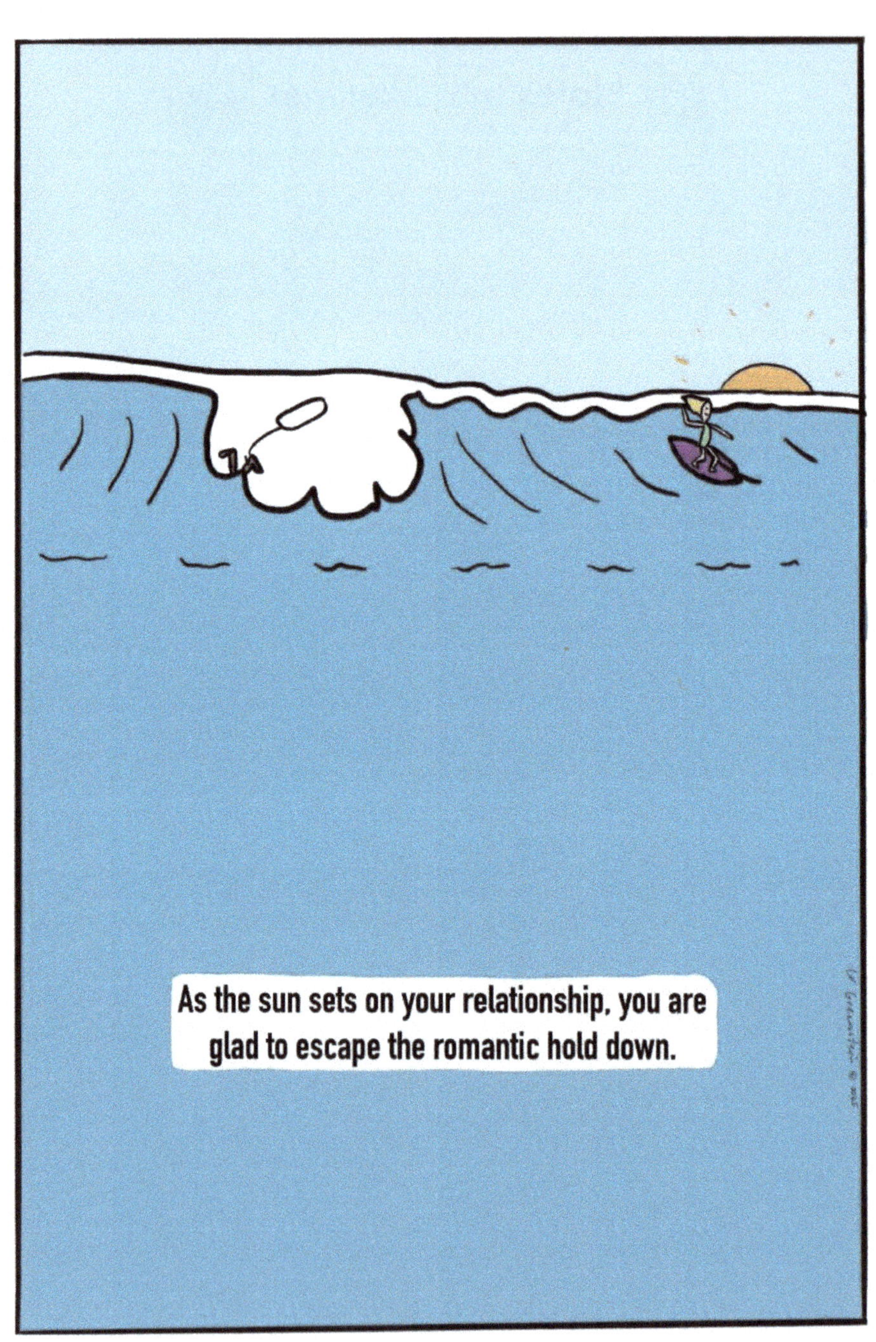

As the sun sets on your relationship, you are
glad to escape the romantic hold down.

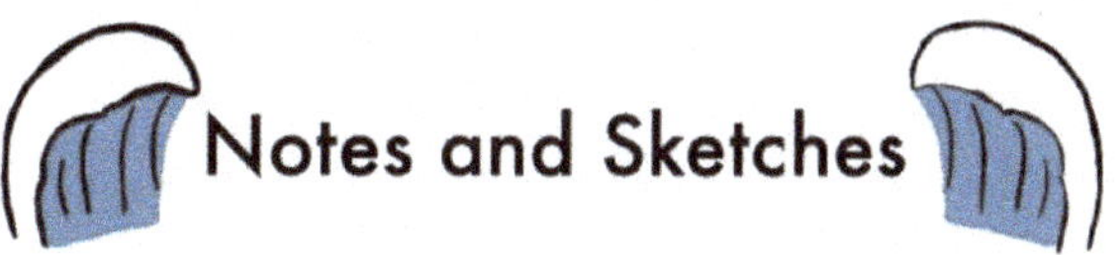

Notes and Sketches

You know you are in a surf town when...

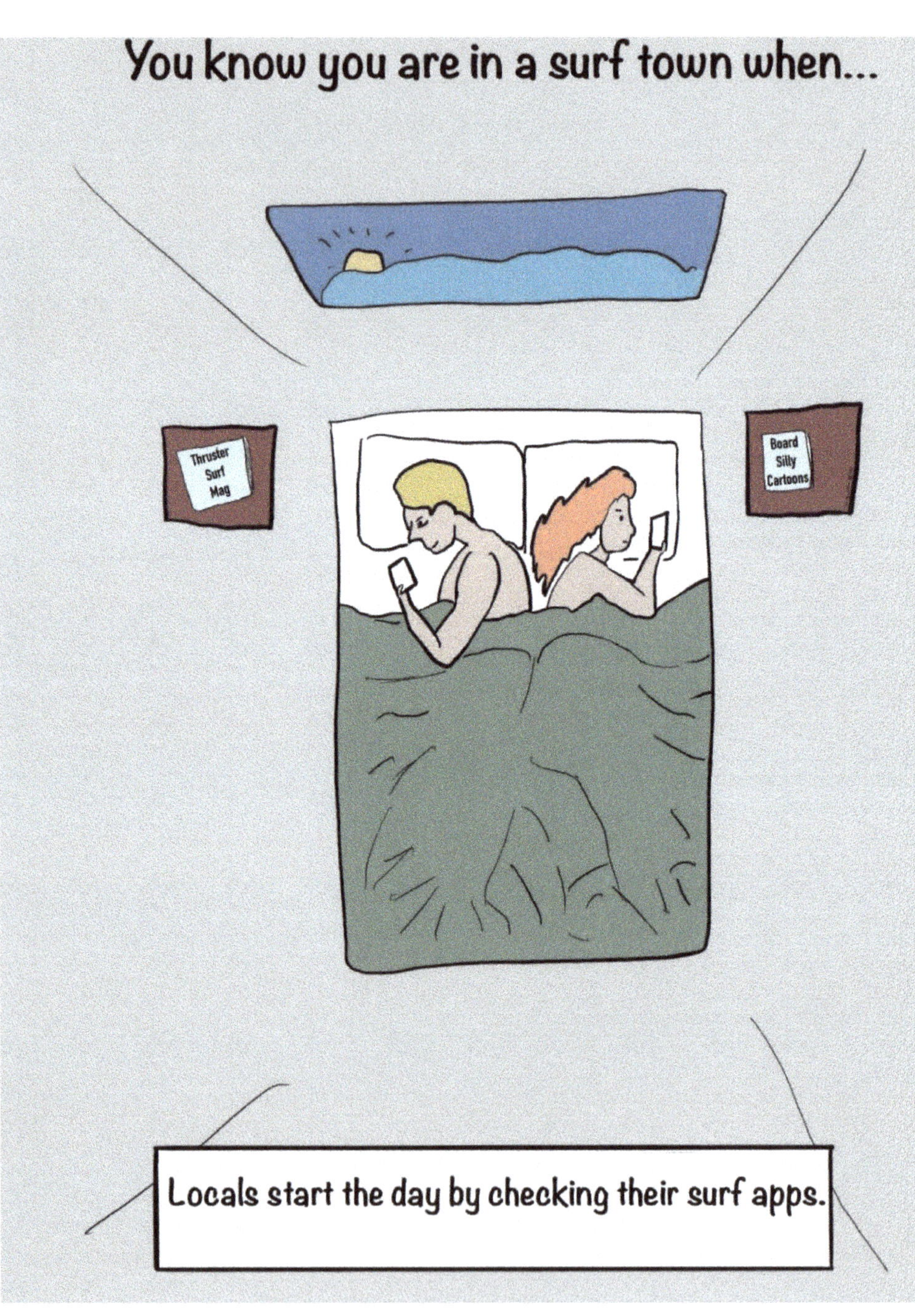

Locals start the day by checking their surf apps.

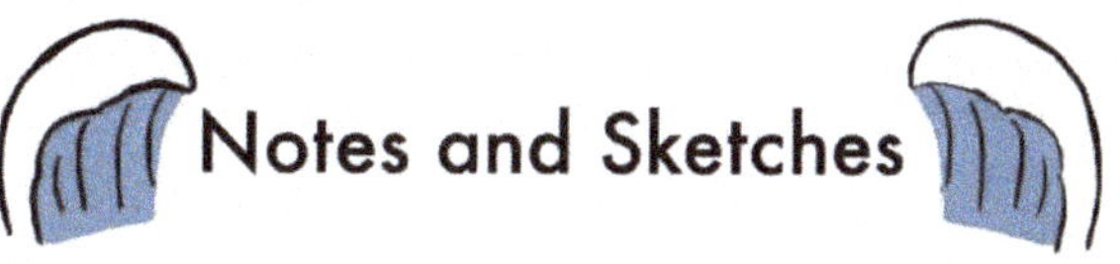

Notes and Sketches

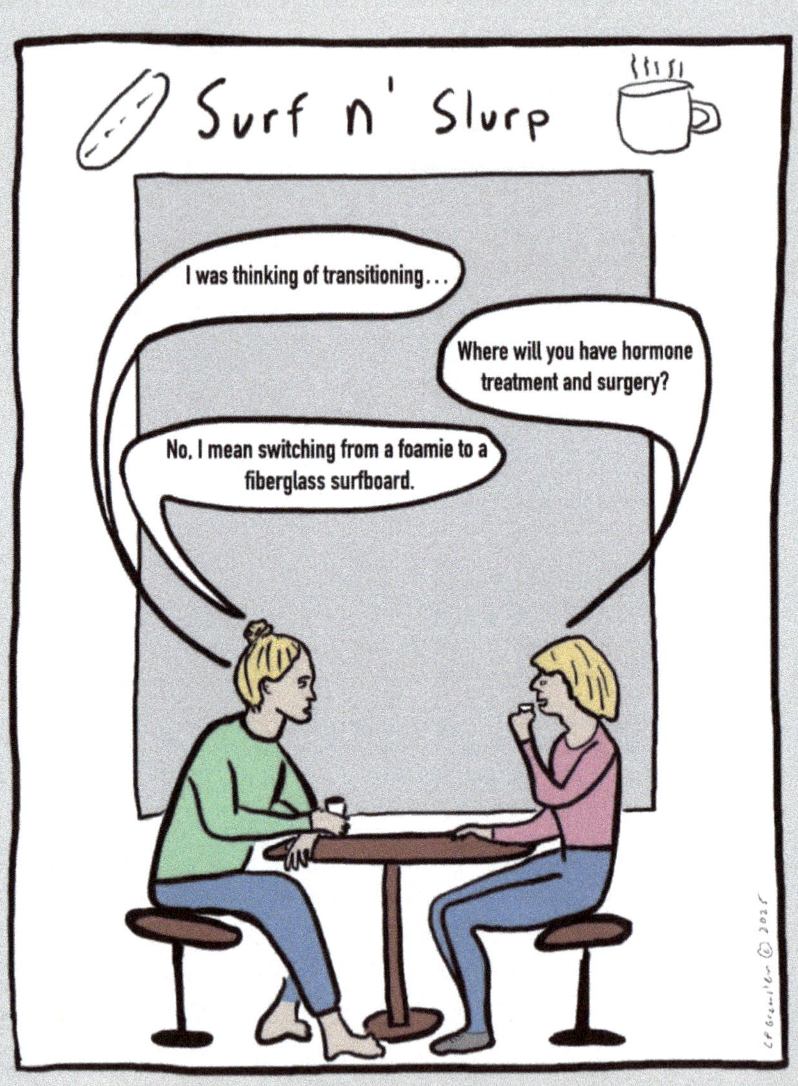

Words take on a new meaning.

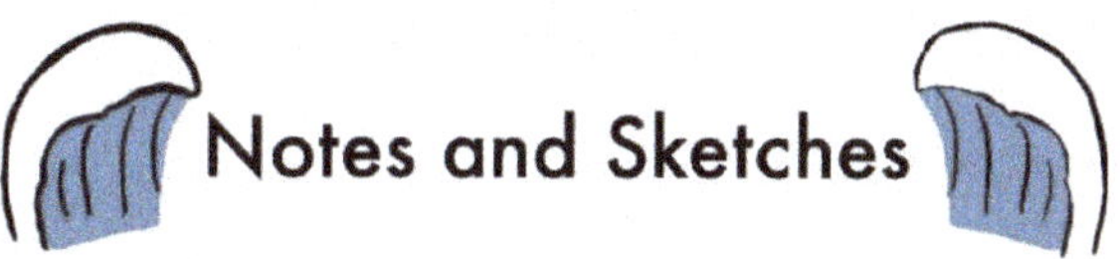

Notes and Sketches

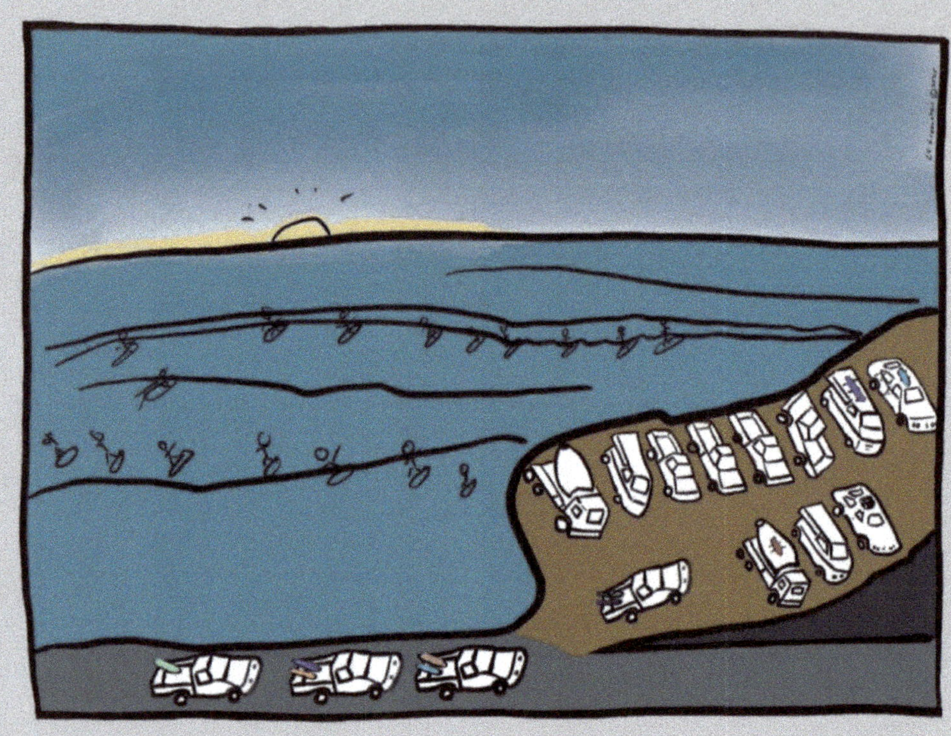

Residents do not want daylight savings time
because they want to surf before work
(especially tradespeople).

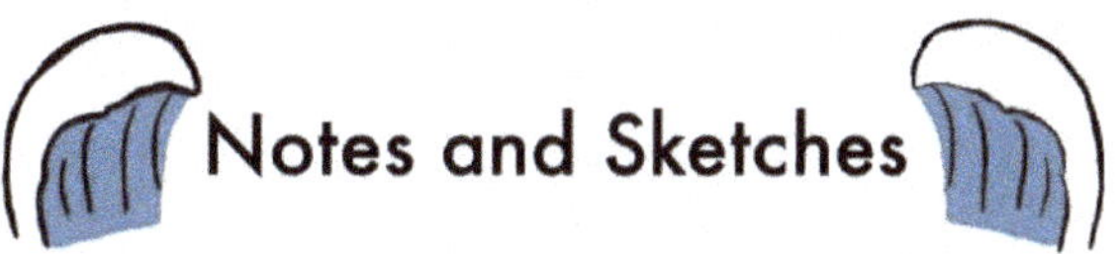
Notes and Sketches

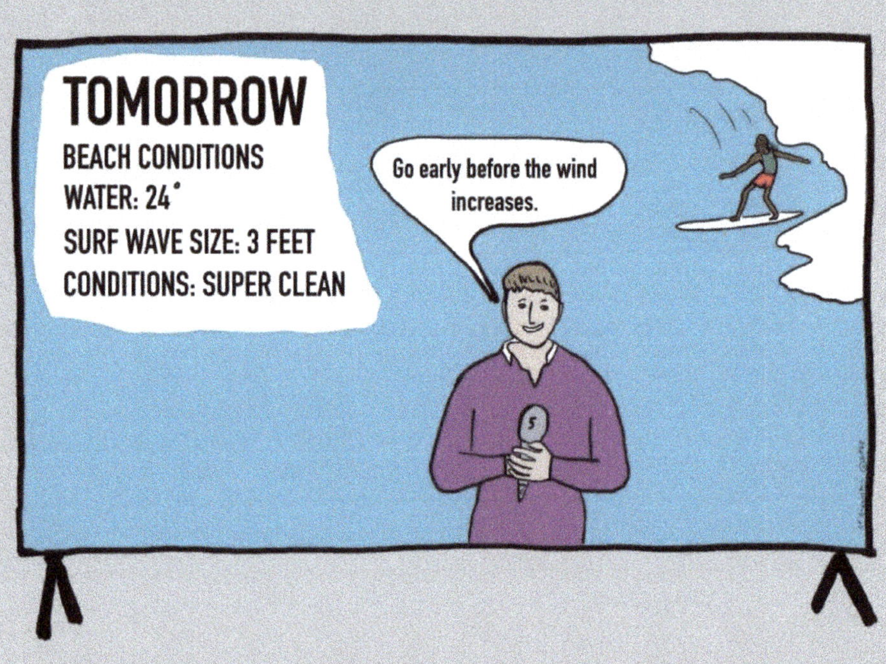

The weather reports include conditions for surfers.

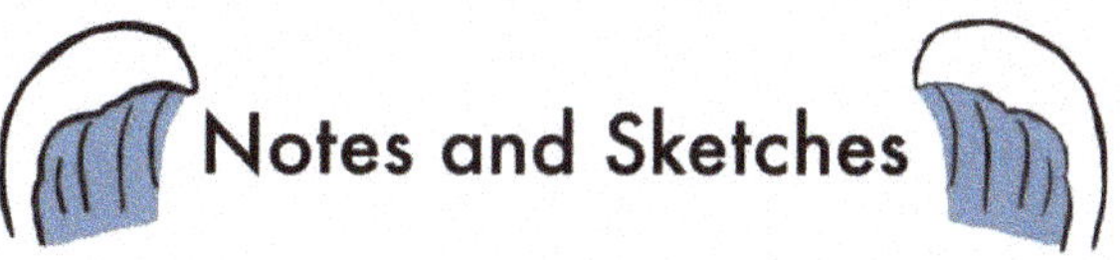

Notes and Sketches

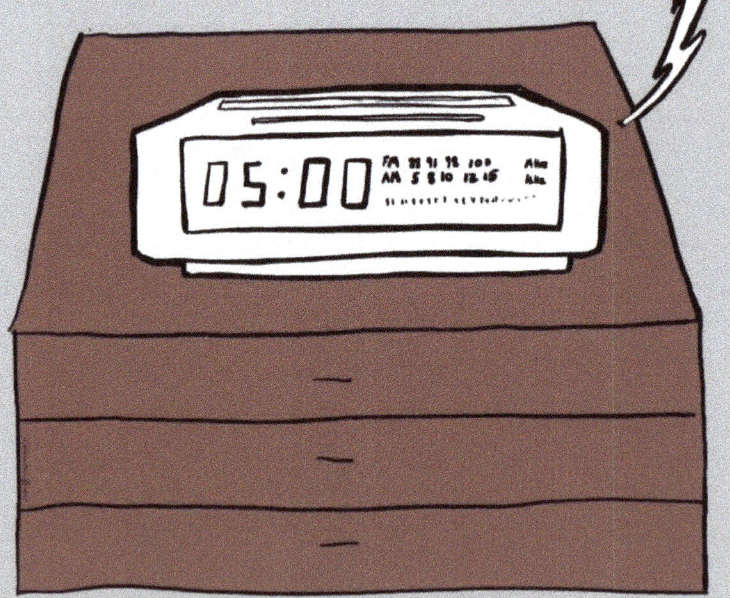

The surf reports contain the number of surfers at each beach.

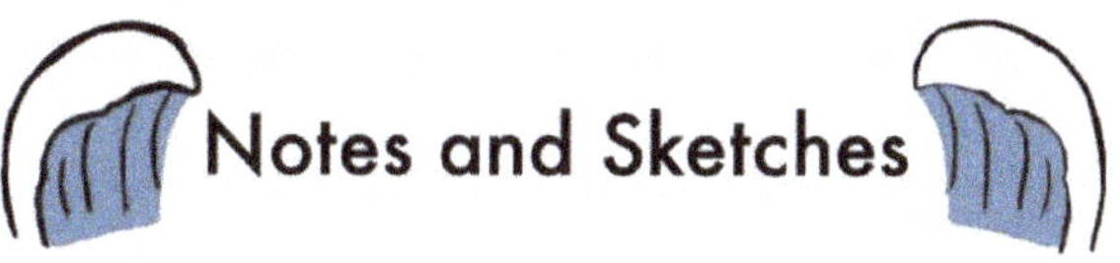

Notes and Sketches

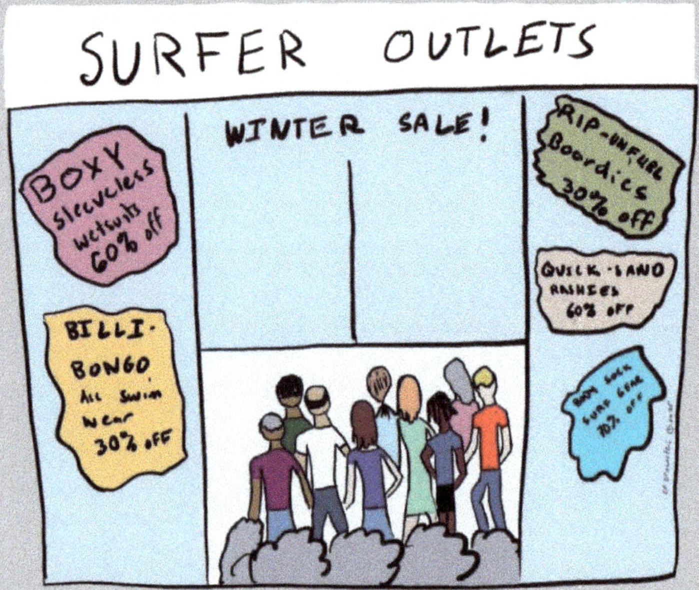

Sales take place at the change of seasons instead of on holidays.

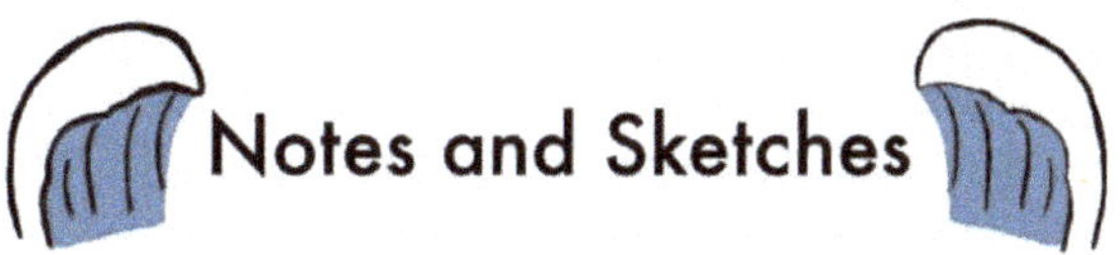

Notes and Sketches

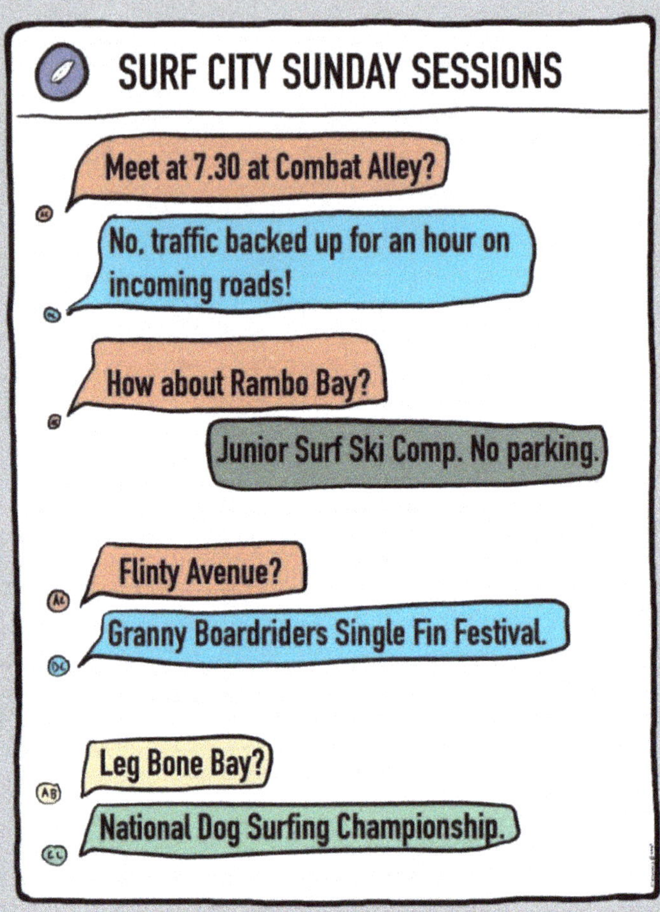

Traffic, parking and crowds are a consideration when meeting for a surf.

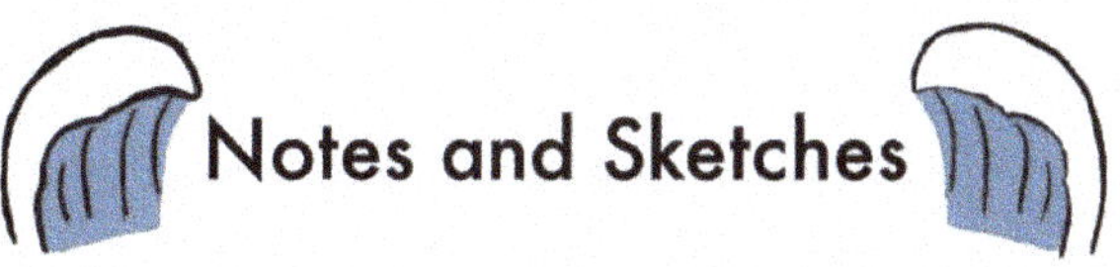

Notes and Sketches

Locals have an unusual interpretation of weather reports.

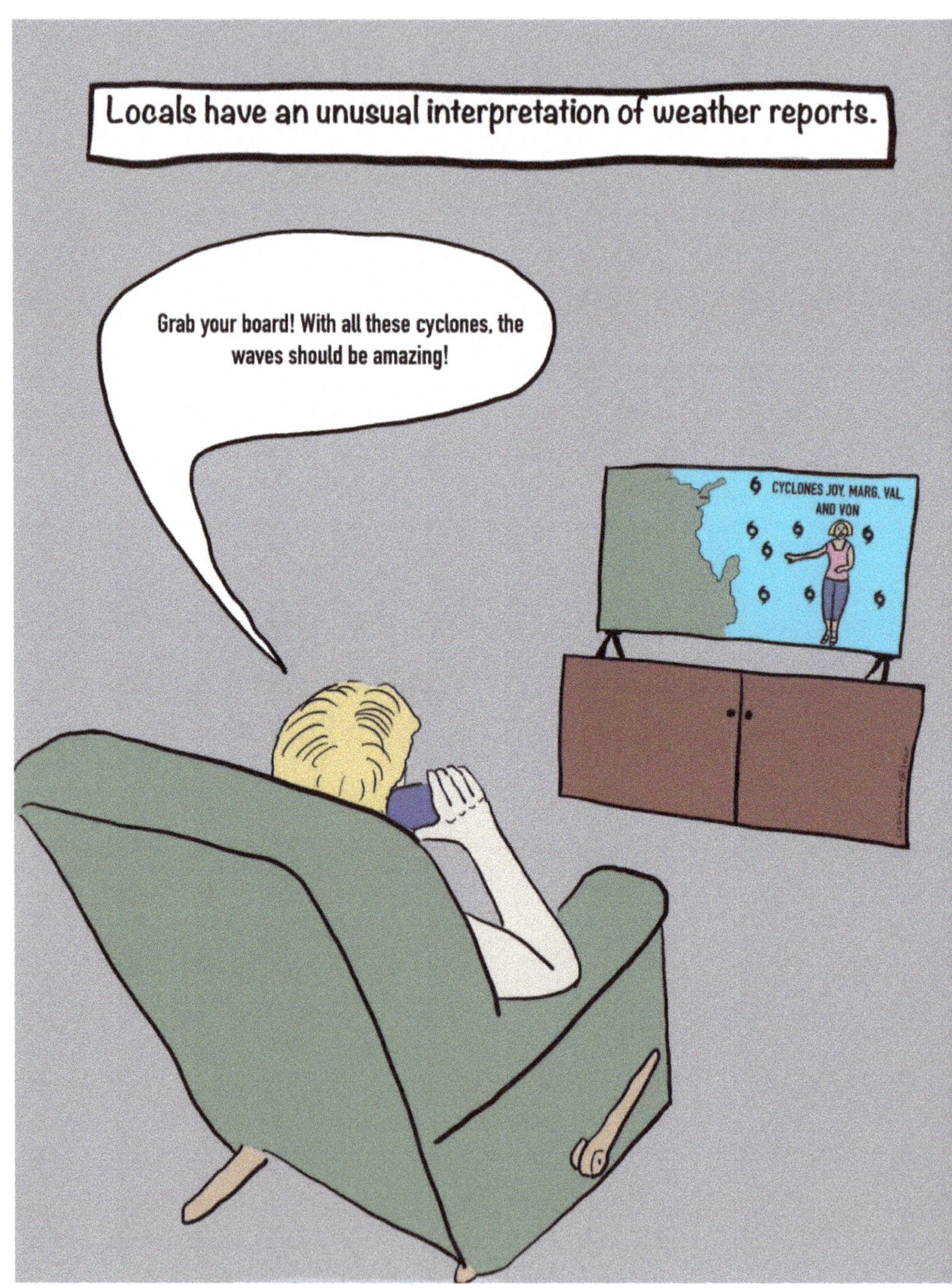

Grab your board! With all these cyclones, the waves should be amazing!
CYCLONES JOY, MARG, VAL, AND VON

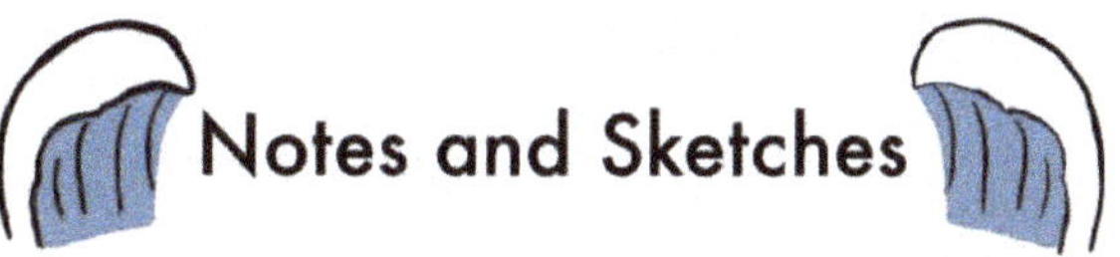
Notes and Sketches

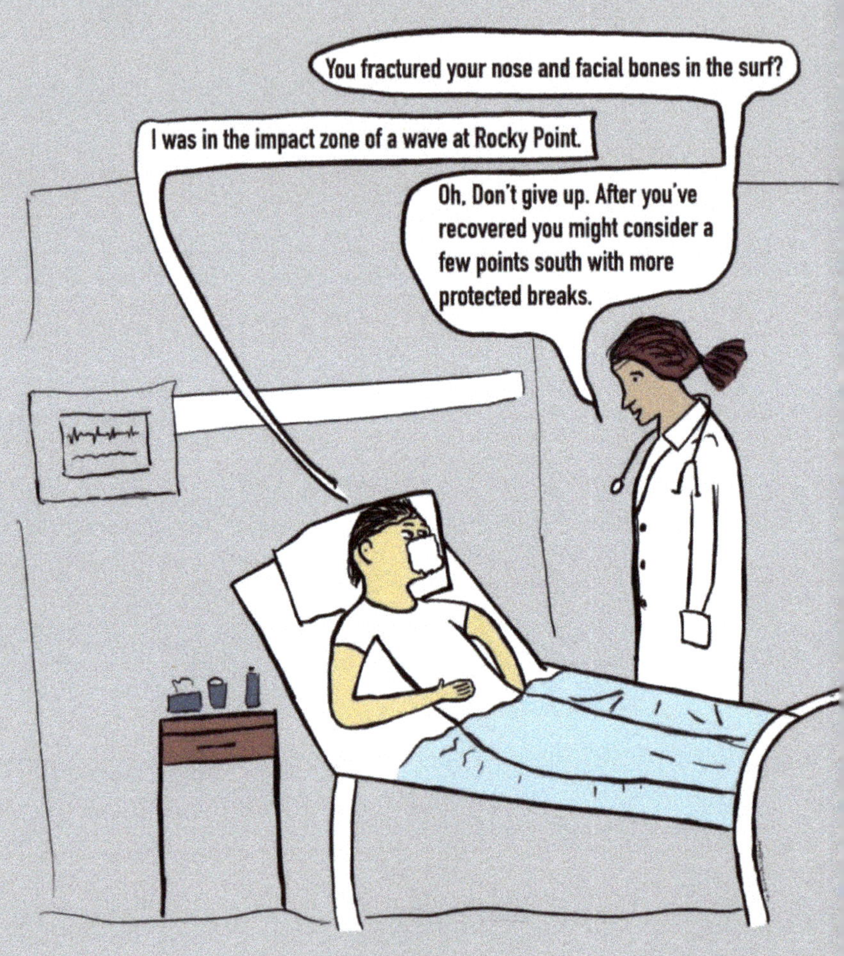

Surfing figures in hospital discussions.

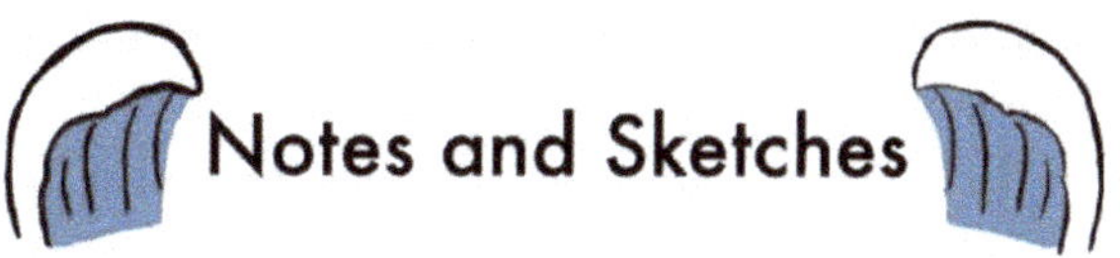

Notes and Sketches

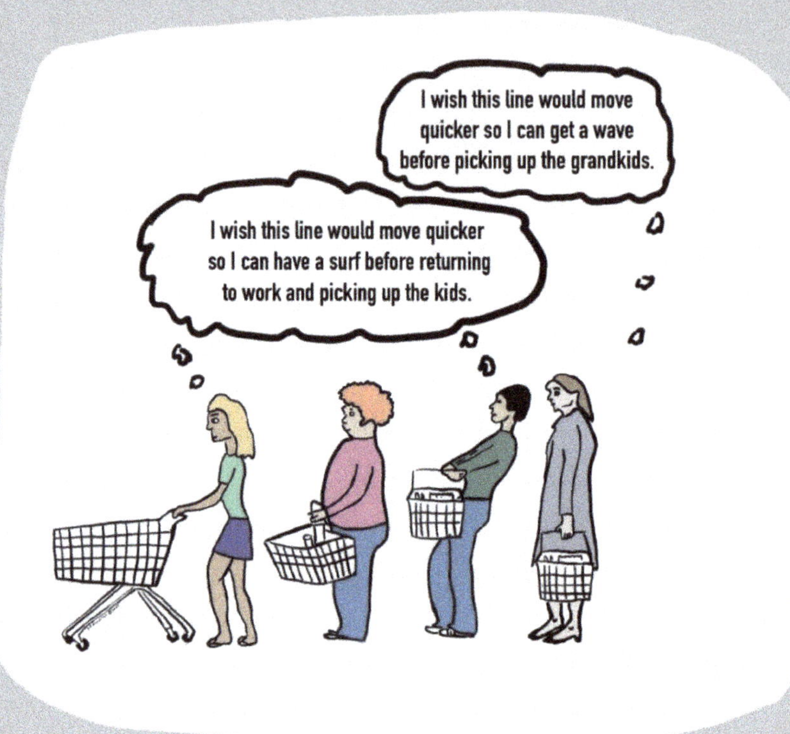

People are preoccupied while running errands.

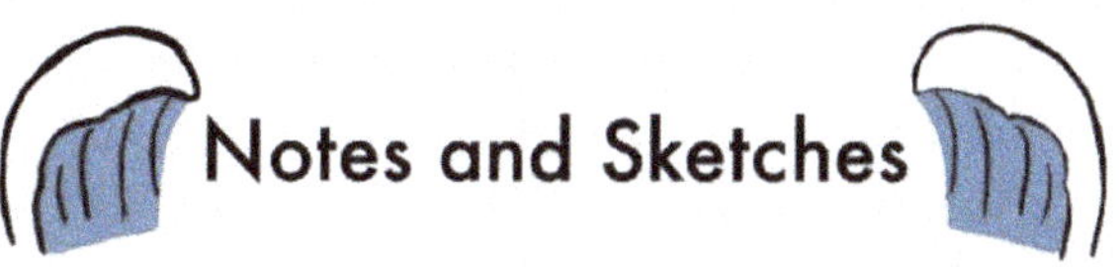
Notes and Sketches

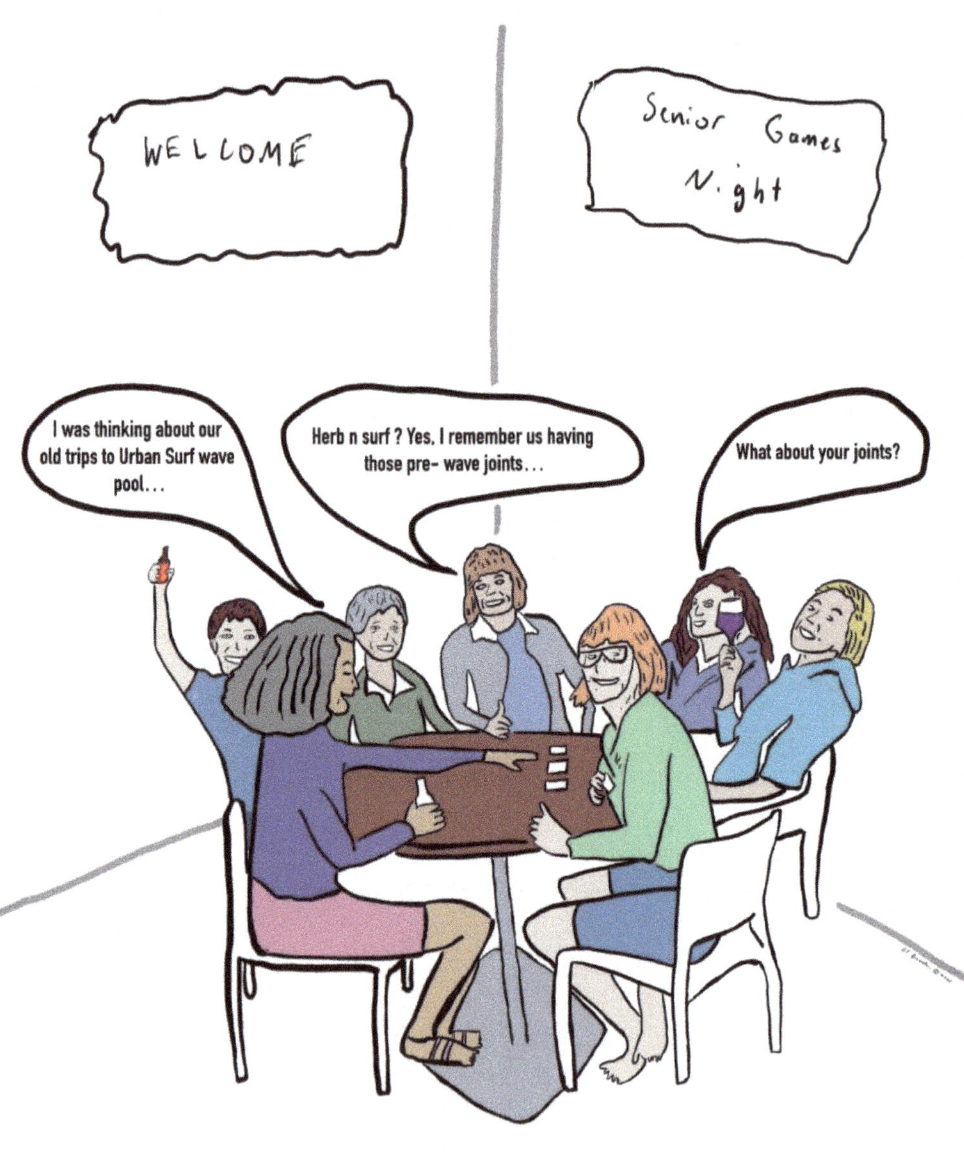

Conversations drift toward surfing
during social gatherings.

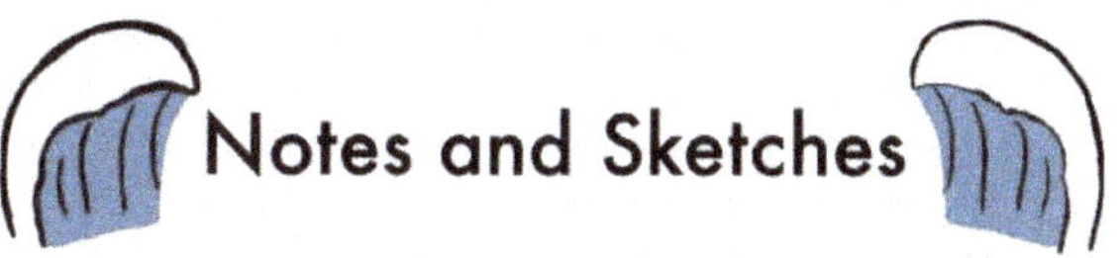

Notes and Sketches

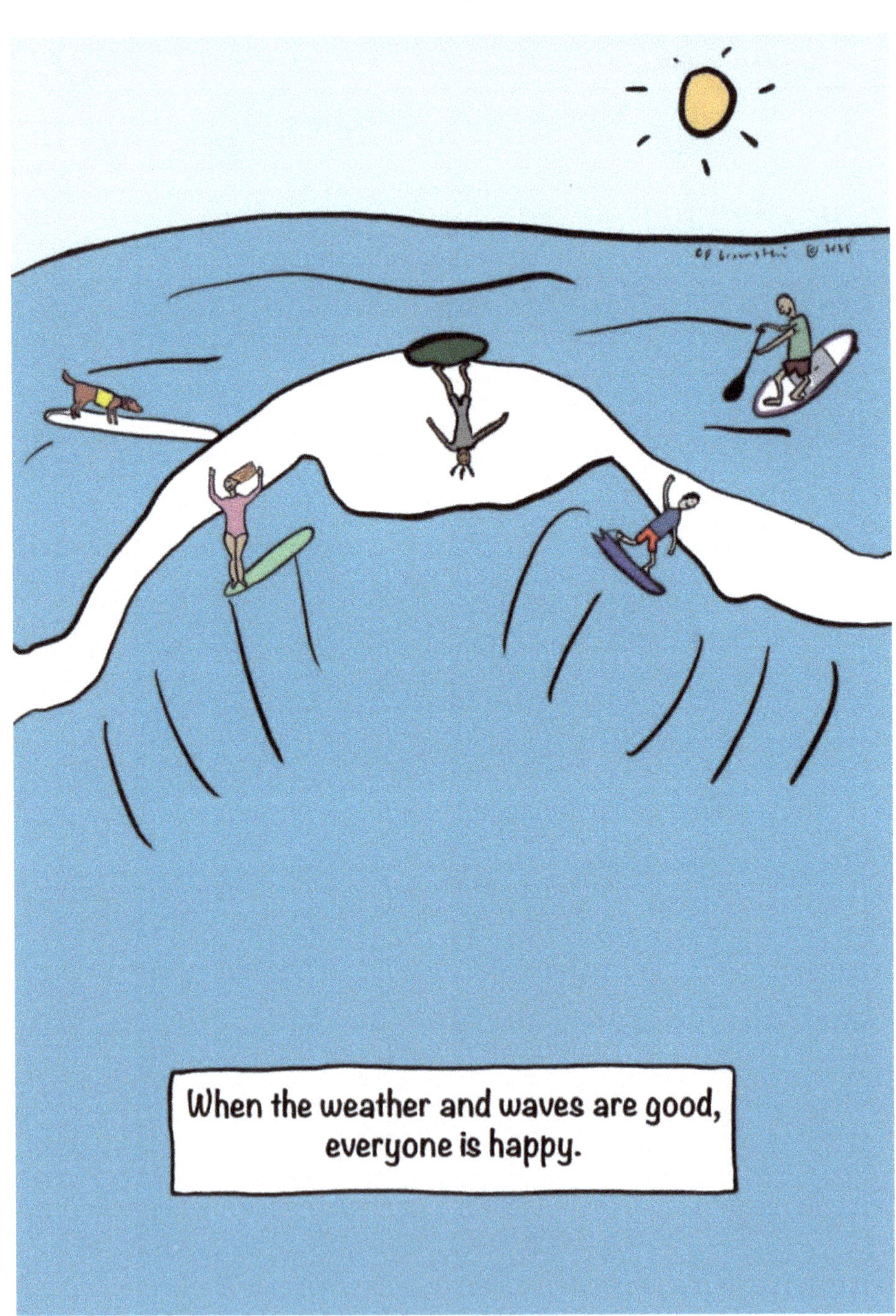

When the weather and waves are good,
everyone is happy.

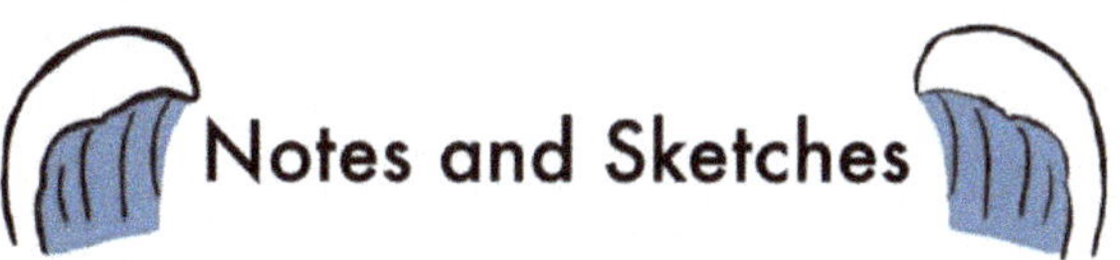

Notes and Sketches

Acknowledgements

I wish to thank my partner Kim for her patience and perspective; her frequent peals of laughter while viewing this project were as pleasurable as a good wave. I would also like to thank my publisher Helen Iles for her helpfulness and advice, staff from my local computer store for their technical advice on graphic art and drawing apps, my surf buddies - especially Gidget Lea, Spring Chickens Helzie, Marg, Von, Joy, Zita, Valerie, Kay, Evie, Sue, Dani, Maxine, Connie, Lindy, Sandy and Izzy – as well as other aquatic and land-based friends for their true-life adventures, enthusiasm and sense of humour.